Icons
of a Dreaming Heart

ICONS

OF A

DREAMING HEART

THE ART AND PRACTICE
OF DREAM-CENTERED LIVING

Renée Coleman

Foreword by Robert Sardello

GOLDENSTONE PRESS | *Benson, North Carolina*

Published by Goldenstone Press
P.O. Box 7
Benson, North Carolina 27504
www.goldenstonepress.com

ISBN: 978-0-9832261-9-2

Cover artwork: Sleeping Venus of Malta carved in stone,
found at the entrance to the the Hypogeum.

Cover and book design: Eva Leong Casey / Lee Nichol

Printed in USA

GOLDENSTONE PRESS

GOLDENSTONE PRESS seeks to make original spiritual thought available as a force of
individual, cultural, and world revitalization. The press is an integral dimension of
the work of the School of Spiritual Psychology. The mission of the School includes
restoring the book as a way of inner transformation and awakening to spirit. We recognize that secondary thought and the reduction of books to sources of information
and entertainment as the dominant meaning of reading places in jeopardy the unique
character of writing as a vessel of the human spirit. We feel that the continuing
emphasis of such a narrowing of what books are intended to be needs to be balanced
by writing, editing, and publishing that emphasizes the act of reading as entering into
a magical, even miraculous spiritual realm that stimulates the imagination and makes
possible discerning reality from illusion in the world. The editorial board of Goldenstone Press is committed to fostering authors with the capacity of creative spiritual
imagination who write in forms that bring readers into deep engagement with an inner transformative process rather than being spectators to someone's speculations. A
complete catalogue of all our books may be found at *www.goldenstonepress.com*. The
web page for the School of Spiritual Psychology is *www.spiritualschool.org*.

10 9 8 7 6 5 4 3 2 1

Contents

Acknowledgements

It is with a deep sense of gratitude that I recognize those who have supported me in the writing of this book. First, my husband, Albert Erdynast, who felt the full impact of my preoccupation and involvement with this work, yet who always supported me with patience, love, and encouragement. Thank you for being the stalwart guardian of my gate.

Next, I would like to thank our four children—Marie-Claire, Esmé, Didier, and Jack, the best things I ever made with eggs—for their understanding and enduring support, and for their willingness to step, ever gracefully, into the space created by their mother's physical absence. How did I ever get so lucky?

I would also like to thank those dedicated and courageous dreamers whose dreaming presences are woven throughout this work—without them, and without their willingness to be "borrowed" in this way, this book would not be possible; I am immensely grateful, and each and every one of them shares in the writing credit. They are: Ralph Albi, Leon Aliski, Jacque Allen, Maureen Benoit, Marlene Bernstein, Joei Bidwell, Jane Buttrey, Jason D'Ercola, Steve Donahue, Laurie Jacobs, Cesar Jass, Camillia Johnson, Tina Landrum, Ocean Lum, Suzanne Loesch, Karen Maleck-Whiteley, Kevin Maynard, Jane Monteagle, Jennie Moran, Penny Randall, Faith Rutherford, Ann Traver Mukherjee, and Dorothy Ward (whose almost lifelong devotion to all that I am in the world deserves special mention). Special mention must also be given to Chaplain Maryloyola Yettke and all of the unflinchingly honest women at California Institute for Women who, though they shall remain anonymously credited here, never cease to amaze me—all of them likewise share credit for writing this book.

A big thank you also goes out to Christine Downing for her love, her on going support, and that special knack she has for evoking my emulative envy.

My gratitude also extends to Eva Casey for the book's design, and to Lee Nichol, a truly remarkable editor, for his careful reading and brilliant suggestions, and for so much more. May there be many more opportunities for us to collaborate in years to come.

Finally, and most especially, to Robert Sardello, the book's midwife, for his tireless devotion. From his first, almost casual suggestion, "Why don't you write a book on dreams?" to his selfless dedication to all that is required in order to bring a work like this into being, Robert has been so much more than a mentor and guide, he's been an inspiration. Working with him is not only an incredible privilege—it's an absolute joy. James Hillman once said that "whatever Robert Sardello touches breaks open with startling new meaning." It seems to me that this is because whatever Robert Sardello touches, he makes it shine—as though he lends some of his luster and brilliance and the light of his being to all that he comes into contact with, with love and grace, with humility, and with an enormous generosity of spirit. For this and for all that he is endeavoring in the world, I am truly thankful.

The author and publisher would like to acknowledge permission to use all or part of the following:

Antonio Machado, "The Wind, One Brilliant Day," from *Times Alone— Selected Poems of Antonio Machado*, translated by Robert Bly (c) 1983. Reprinted by permission of Wesleyan University Press.

Hafiz, "I Got Kin" and "Too Beautiful" from the Penguin publication *The Gift, Poems by Hafiz*, copyright 1999 Daniel Ladinsky and used with his permission.

Jalāl ad-Dīn Muhammad Rūmī, "Listening" and "Love Dogs," from the Maypop publication *Say I am You Rumi: Poetry Interspersed with Stories of Rumi and Shams*, translated by Coleman Barks and John Moyne, (c) 1994 Coleman Barks and used with his permission.

"Annunciation," from *The Kingdom of Ordinary Time* by Marie Howe. Copyright (c) 2008 by Marie Howe. Used by permission of W. W. Norton & Company, Inc.

"Sometimes a Man Stands Up During Summer" (8 lines) from *Selected Poems of Rainer Maria Rilke, A Translation from the German and Commentary* by Robert Bly. Copyright (c) 1981 by Robert Bly. Reprinted by permission of HarperCollins Publishers.

Excerpt from "A Poet's Advice to Students," Copyright (c) 1955, 1965 by the Trustees for the E. E. Cummings Trust. Copyright (c) 1958, 1965 by George J. Firmage, from *A Miscellany Revised* by E. E. Cummings, Edited by George J. Firmage. Used by permission of Liveright Publishing Corporation.

Source for the following:

William Stafford, "Being a Person," from *Even in Quiet Places*, Confluence Press, 2010.

FOREWORD

Words and language are so very interesting because they are useful, portable, and seemingly able to cross nearly all boundaries of understanding. Renée Coleman writes completely directly, openly, and without a hint of jargon or "specialized" language. One only has to be interested in the theme of dreams and dreaming to be able to pick up this book and seem to readily understand what she has written. At the most immediate level, this understanding does occur, and *Icons of a Dreaming Heart* can be deeply appreciated at that level. But there is so much more to this book. A brief foreword may be not only necessary, but also helpful in alerting you, dear reader, to orient yourself with the kind of attention needed to be fully engaged with this writing; and even more importantly, allowing this speaking to fully enter into the very depths of your being— with more and more understanding with each reading.

There are years and years of work backing the writing of this book. Realizing that the very substance of our writer's life has gone into the making of this work lends it a proper seriousness, though the tone of every sentence is equally joy-filled. You can immediately tell that this writing cannot be separated from the very being of the author. Thus, there will likely be a moment of hesitation before opening the first page, and a bit of an inner caution throughout your reading. I am not suggesting anything even remotely like fear, though you are approaching the truly unknown. Past categories of understanding fall away, and the best approach is noticing that good reading is first of all good listening. So, the suggested caution is not one of holding back, but of really letting go and letting the speaking of this book work on you, within you, as it will surely do. I speak with confidence on this point, for *Icons of a Dreaming Heart* has radically altered who I am.

You may feel deeply "jolted" as you read this dramatic book carefully. It is like being thrown into radical disorientation, while at the same time discovering an inner compass pointing to—and even placing you directly within—a different domain, a different reality that is actually the very depth of what we experience as "everyday reality." One of the wonders of this writing is that while the theme is dreams and working with dreams, the Presences of dreams and the dream worlds are with us all the time, waking and sleeping, though we have never noticed them as always here. We typically only notice them when they assert themselves in ways that squeeze an emotional response or a puzzlement out of us when we wake in the morning. The comfortable isolation of believing that dreams are just strange firings of errant brain circuitry, or that they are complex and symbolic rebuses that can only be interpreted by a psychoanalyst, or that there are books which help you to "know" what dreams mean—whatever you may think that dreams are and mean—all this completely dissolves as you proceed from chapter to chapter. The question of interpretation disappears.

Every line of this writing demonstrates that dreams are far, far more than strange visitations of the night. They are the dramatic "doings" of worlds beyond us that are completely interwoven with this world—and yet beyond our usual perceptions and thinking. Not only the "doings" of worlds, but also Presences within those worlds, purposely acting, creating Presences, who are constituting, every moment, what we call "reality"— though we lack any sense whatsoever that reality is not an "it," but a "Who" and a "They."

Such a forewarning foreword can and does sound pretty strange, and you have to experience the dream worlds through the vision of Renée Coleman yourself for the realization to dawn, and such realization is as close as what you are holding in your hands. You don't have to go "looking" for soul Presences as your read—I do not want to "over-prepare" you, for then you would miss the event because it has been cognized rather than realized as revelation.

That "you" in a dream who is always experienced in the depth of sleeping is not you, certainly not literally you, and not just a kind of pictorial representation of you either—it is you and simultaneously another "you." Even more, a dream, say, of Uncle Harry, is more than a jumbled up memory that has somehow combined with the full stomach of last night's dinner. It is the Presence of Uncle Harry! He is really present, though in a mostly unrecognizable form if you don't know how to listen. And we don't, so we immediately convert his reality as imaginal being, as a spirit-soul individual, into what we already know about Uncle Harry. Then, of course, dreams make no sense because we have tried to force a different but present reality into our only known version of reality—and it just does not work.

Engaging with dreaming on its own terms is not something I have read about extensively, nor am I concocting this view and imposing it on what Renée Coleman has written. It is not exactly her "view" either, not if you take viewpoint to mean a new theory of dreams. Rather, the description here of dream figures as actual Presences very accurately portrays exactly what occurs over and over again, dream example after dream example, in this book. Both the key and the essence of Renée Coleman's writing is encountered when you enter into the dramatic unfolding, first as a dream is told, and then as the characters, scenes, and action of each dream begin to reveal their "substance." They feel "real,"every bit as real as something physically present, though the reality here is imaginal presence.

You will encounter this term—imaginal—multiple times in this writing, and it is one of the few terms that might be unfamiliar. Dr. Coleman places what occurs as she and the dream groups meet and engage with the dream stories people relate, within a background of

the Archetypal Psychology of James Hillman and the extraordinary
work of Henry Corbin and his development of a very clear sense of the
"imaginal" realm as within early esoteric Sufism. These references help
locate the intellectual setting of this book. But, this background stays
there—in the background, a kind of intellectual resonance should any
reader wish to pursue it. In reading, the revealing of imaginal reality
occurs, directly, immediately, bodily, and worldly.

The many dream Presences Dr. Coleman embracingly encourages
to emerge in her masterful listening as people tell their dreams, and then
a creative repeating of the dreams in such a way that those Presences are
invited into the room and now into your room as you read, is a living
demonstration of the realm of the imaginal. The reader gets to see, feel,
touch, and experience fully the very working and existence of this ever-
present fabric that actually holds together and makes "actual" all that
we experience. Her work with dreams individualizes that vast and all-
pervasive creative-making of soul reality and makes it possible for us to
move into this reality, now consciously, as if into a brand new abode of
life—life immeasurably expanded and deepened.

This experience of becoming more than we ever knew possible
establishes this book as paradigm-shattering and paradigm-creating.
The implications are astounding. I will not take the easy route, though,
and stop at mildly suggesting that at last we have a substantial sense
of the significance of dreaming, something that has been lost for ages,
and once lost, trampled on by every possible psychological theory. The
significance of what Renée has done, which is a wholly practical working
with groups of people who bring their dreams into the center of the room
and let them step from mouth into reality, goes even further than this—
much, much further.

Most scientists (and psychologists who play like they are scientists)
and, as well, the pragmatic rest of us who simply live a kind of forgetful

existence, like to keep clear dividing lines between what is "real"—
which is described as what can be sensed, measured, and mutually
agreed upon—and the "other side," characterized by those artists of
every conceivable type who stand in and for and delight in the symbolic,
mystical, spiritual realities and the more or less "spooky," as seen by the
folks on the literal side of the line. It does not take very long to discover
in reading this book that such lines of division are due to intellectual
constructions and simply do not adequately describe immediate
experience. More than that, we humans have perhaps come to the place
where the cessation of world destruction requires the ability to traverse
these two domains as one originating place and orientation. In her
research, practical work with groups, writing, and living, Dr. Coleman
has managed to expand the border area and keep it open for everyone
to explore.

Not just explore, though. This vast border-area, where we might
well conjecture the "realities" on either side are being brought into
existence, itself undergoes creative transformations by being attended to
in the ways entered into in this book. It is this event that constitutes the
extreme import and significance of the writing.

The coming about of a "new creation" is quietly spoken of in this
book; mostly it just happens and you can be aware that indeed this is
happening. To try and say what this creation is about, think of any one
of the concrete instances of dream work in the writing. If you read and
come away feeling , "Well, that was interesting, exciting, and really helps
me with my life," and that is it, then something of extreme importance
has slipped by you, and you have fallen back into the trap of self-
centeredness. Fallback is inevitable, but stepping fully into the content
and form and action of what our author has created produces un-erasable
resonance. Something radically other than self-centeredness shines
through the book and will begin radiating from your being. You can feel

it; so do others. Once the core of the imaginal worlds and Presences has been felt, there is the beginning of an ascendency of Wisdom.

You may well read this book and "know" what it says quite immediately. Wisdom unfolds in proper timing, suitable to who you are and what you are able to experience. Wisdom is wordless, at first, so the resonances of a close and caring reading are felt bodily, and in our sensing and perceiving. Right after reading *Icons of a Dreaming Heart*, you are apt to notice a kind of body-sense-perception expansion. That goes away, but it is something like the "seeding" of the unfolding of Wisdom. You can, for example, notice your dreams in a completely different way, befriending them rather than either dismissing them or interpreting them.

The dream work of the Dr. Coleman's groups is itself a training, perhaps even an initiation into the capacity of imagination, the organ for perceiving imaginal reality. Such an initiation is not any kind of learning—intellectual, practical, pragmatic, or physical. It is an alchemical transforming of our very being in which more of the whole of our being—body, soul, spirit, world—is "dipped," again and again, into the invisible Presences who have been invited by acts of erotic heart-love. Like love everywhere and of all kinds, mutuality rules. That is, the dream workers and the dream Presences themselves are both altered by what they undergo. While we are accustomed to at least hope for our transformation, here in this writing we see that transformation is also an action. We discover in an immediate way that the imaginal Presences of a dream transform, become more than they were when they showed up in the imaginal dream world. Resonances of dreams begin to show up in the events of our lives, in our perceptions in the world.

It is possible to carefully describe exactly how the unfolding of the dream-wisdom occurs in more esoteric and philosophical terms. Henry Corbin describes this kind of spiritual alchemy in his many writings, particularly clearly in *Spiritual Body, Celestial Earth*. He does so, however, through his eloquent descriptions of the work of the spiritual masters of

Islamic Sufism. The revelation that something like this transformation of invisible Presences occurs when working imaginally with dream work and guidance as Dr. Coleman describes, is nothing short of revolutionary and mind-bending. It suggests that we are with dreams for the sake of the dreams rather than for the sake of the dreamers' betterment. It can be conceived as also for the sake of the improvement of the dreamer, but in a decidedly different manner than trying to "help" a dreamer in a direct way, which inevitably leads right back into self-centeredness. Through the kind of dream work described here, we become "better" in indescribable and invisible but palpable ways – because we are registering the furtherance of larger creating taking place. This completely new way of understanding "betterment" is an inevitable and unavoidable conclusion that dawns slowly, one not attained through thinking, but bodily experienced through engaging the dream world and dream Presences in the manner described in what you are about to read.

The real "secret" of Dr. Renee Coleman—a completely open secret, available to anyone—is that imaginal thinking, imaginal action, imaginal being comes about only and exclusively through the action of love. Not sentimental, emotional, or even a so-called "higher" kind of love, but through the love of the heart, which is exactly the same as the thinking of the heart and the imagining heart. It is a new mode of consciousness, available to anyone, fostered by the dream Presences themselves. Through this kind of love-action-thinking, subtle dream Presences become more substantial; that is, they transform in the direction of spiritual substance while we, in our substance as carriers, holders, and caring listeners become substance more spiritualized. What more could anyone ever want from a book?

Robert Sardello
August 2012

There is a marvelous poem by Rainer Maria Rilke entitled *Sometimes a Man Stands Up During Supper*. It goes like this:

Sometimes a man stands up during supper
and walks outdoors, and keeps on walking,
because of a church that stands somewhere in the East.

And his children say blessings on him as if he were dead.

And another man, who remains inside his own house,
Dies there, inside the dishes and in the glasses,
So that his children have to go out far into the world
Toward that same church, which he forgot.[1]

This poem gives an over-the-shoulder glance at the way things have so far unfolded for the Western "either/or" imagination—either we leave hearth and home on a quest, or we stay home and relinquish the quest. But now it's as though all the old ways are crumbling. Now, it seems that the "church in the East" in Rilke's poem—the one that has been forgotten and is trying to be remembered—is right here *at* the supper table, *with* the children, and *inside* those same dishes and glasses. In other words, the glasses and the dishes and the children *are* the church in the East. So it's not the objects of our focus that need to be transformed, but rather our way of seeing them, of experiencing them, so that instead of focusing merely on the surface of things, materially, we begin to see through them, with them, to the light of ensouled being.

INTRODUCTION

The Burning Bush is only a brushwood fire if
it is merely perceived by the sensory organs.

— Henry Corbin

My twelve-year-old recently asked me to help her study for an upcoming biology exam. Using a series of flashcards that she had prepared specifically, I called out various "biological" terms as she endeavored to recite their definitions. We were sailing through the circulatory system when I got to a card with the word "heart" written across the front of it. Immediately flooded with all sorts of heart-related images, I was struck then as I turned the card over and listened to my daughter deliver its so-called definition.

"A myogenic muscular organ found in all animals with a circulatory system (including all vertebrates)," she said, hesitating while trying to recollect the next part, " . . . that is responsible for pumping blood throughout the blood vessels by repeated, rhythmic contractions."

"Correct," I said, moving the card to the bottom of the pile. Then, unable to stop myself, "But of course it's not *only* that."

"Mom," she said, rolling her eyeballs with exaggerated exasperation.

"Well, we all know that the heart is a physical organ that has shape, motion, volume, heat, and rhythm," I said. "That it's a pump . . ."

"Mom!"

"But why are they not also telling you that it's a sensory organ, attuned to the intuitive transmission of information way beyond the scope of your other sensory organs?"

"Just move onto the next card, would ya, Ma?"

"And that it is a perceptive organ," I continued, pretending not to notice her consternation. "Uniquely receptive to the ideals, images, and archetypes that invest material forms with life and meaning. Why are they not teaching you that?"

"Because it's a seventh grade biology test," my daughter said, her eyebrows folding over each other.

"But this is biology!" I insisted. "The heart is an indispensable organ of perception and moral judgment."

"Dad!" she called out then, snatching the flash cards dramatically from my hands as I feigned innocence. "What?" I chuckled.

"Dad!" she called out again.

"You'll be back!" I shouted after my daughter as she stomped upstairs to find her father—a man who is always a more reliable and reasonable study partner than I, but not nearly as fun. Or at least that's what I tell myself.

As highlighted by this little story, a cultural tendency currently exists that would reduce the heart as an organ to its biological function. Yes, of course the heart is a pump, but it's not *only* a pump. For, in reality, as the Sufis remind us, the heart is also: "Leader of the Body! Friend of the Form! Ruler of the Organs! Proof of the Parts! Seed of the Flesh! . . . The Second Throne of God! The Cap of Light! Yes, ever since Adam was seated upon the dais of vice-regency, it is known that the Throne of God is within the human breast."[2]

Icons of a Dreaming Heart is therefore offered as imaginal corrective to the current reductionism of the heart. For if we are but rightly oriented, dreams and the dreaming way can "organically" develop the heart as an organ of perception. In order for this to occur, however, not only will we be required to concentrate *on* the heart, we will need to learn how to allow ourselves to become concentrated *by* the heart—to allow ourselves to surrender so that we might be *remembered forward by heart*.

Following the tradition set before us by Henry Corbin, that master of the visionary, thinking heart, what follows in these pages is both a *récit*—a term that comes to us from the French, meaning "recital," which seeks to inspire the heart by recitations of life lived in the imaginal— and, in order that we might release the imagination from its current state of captivity, it is likewise an invitation to rediscover the heart as an organ of perception. This work, therefore, is neither a fiction nor an objective history of facts. And it most certainly is not an allegory in which personified figures act as stand-ins for abstract concepts. Instead, it is the soul's own story, told in the first person by way of images. It is, in short, an invitation to vision.

The challenge, therefore, is how to take what unfolds in the dreamtime like a play—an alive, embodied, in-the-room dream drama, and make it directly available to the reader. In other words, a *closet drama*—a play that is designed and written with the intent that it be read rather than performed. What follows in these pages, however, is not scripted dialogue between characters that is intended as a theatrical performance. So in this sense, it is not formally a play. And yet it *is* a drama.

The word "drama" comes from a Greek word meaning "action," which is derived from "to do," or "to act." The enactment of drama in theatre, performed by actors on a stage before an audience, presupposes collaborative modes of production and a collective form of reception. Writing, too, presupposes a collective form of reception, albeit one audience member, that is, one reader, at a time.

The word "theatre" also comes to us from the Greeks; it means "the seeing place." Aristotle took the Mysteries and more or less made them public through the form of drama. Individuals were introduced, taken into, and exposed to something so utterly unknown to them that it crumbled all they knew or thought they knew. It is this "crumbling" that makes soul-seeing possible.

The dreams, imaginal asides, and amblings presented here are a collaborative mode of production that likewise strives to make soul-seeing possible. They are, in a very real sense, the play—the dramatic, theatrical narrative, the warp threads through which all the players, including the writer and the audience, become the weft, weaving the whole thing into being.

Finally, because it is quite contradictory to write "about" the imaginal, the task is to create something that is at the same time an imaginal "doing." For unlike so much of what travesties as theatre these days—which is mostly "spectacle" requiring precious little from the audience beyond the price of the ticket—the dream drama presented here presupposes a much needed, actively engaged and participating audience.

Come therefore humanly to the icons on these pages, as dreamers. Lend yourself uniquely to the dream of the whole thing *as it unfolds.* Allow yourself to be "borrowed," as D.H. Lawrence puts it. The goal here is not to fix things, but to make something new out of what's been given, and to lend ourselves—as individuals, and as a dreaming collective—to the dream of Earth's unfolding.

Part I:

Dreams as Presence

WHO IS VISITING HERE?

"Taking what you said last month about me not sharing any dreams recently," a woman in one of the dream groups I facilitate begins, "I have either a . . ." she pauses, searching for just the right word, "well, it's a sort of nothing . . . a kind of insignificant dream that I can share. And when I say 'dream'—it's really just one image. Or, I can share a recurring dream from my childhood—one that I haven't actually dreamt in many years, though I remain quite curious about it. I mean, I've always thought that it'd be kind of neat to know what that dream means. So the choice is up to you."

From this perspective—which might best be described as the "dream's perspective"—nothing is insignificant. Even if there is "only" one image, it has the same psychic weight as, for example, those epic narratives that unfold like *Ben Hur on Ice*. All dreams and dream images, regardless of their content, have the same psychic weight; the difference lies not in their imaginal significance, but rather in how images penetrate the dreamer. In other words, the difference is in the way that we as dreamers are able to receive the images. And in the way the dream images stick around. Or not. Knowing this and wanting to display it to those gathered, I choose the one-image dream.

"Well," the dreamer begins rather reluctantly, "there's not much to work with. The whole dream lasted less than a minute."

"Let's see," I say by way of encouragement, as everyone in the room settles in to receive the dream.

———

Listen. Can you hear that? It's the sound of deep, inner listening gathering itself to receive the dream. For it's not enough to passively listen to dreams. The endeavor is to actively—that is, receptively—listen, to hear *into* dream images. Rather like the variety of listening that is necessary in improvisational theatre, we want to listen as though creative life entirely depends upon it.

It helps, therefore, to turn our visual attention away from the dreamer, as this tends to be distracting. Additionally, it helps to have an image of active, receptive listening. So, for example, when I settle in to tend a dream, I invariably imagine that I am mounted on the back of a rather high-strung horse—the Horse of Dreams. Together, this Horse of Dreams and I ride out into the Field of Dreams, which is a vast Plain of Possibility, wherein essentially anything and everything can happen, and does. Once there, in a heightened anticipatory state, yet as inwardly still as I can manage to be while on the back of a high-strung horse, I wait with the deep ear inside my chest—the heart's ear—wide open and ready to receive the dream.

For in this realm of possibility, on the back of this noble, majestic creature, with my heart's ear wide open, I am rendered "radically receptive." That is, able to meet and greet the dream on the dream's terms. Out there in the Field of Dreams, the dream's images, the dreamer, and now I begin to have a shared imagination.

When we listen this way, it's important to resist the temptation to look for meaning, to abstract away from receptive listening. Any thought as to what an image might mean invariably renders us unable to be present to the dream as it unfolds. Therefore, as mentioned, it helps to have an image of receptive listening. A human dream-catcher perhaps—a living, breathing, curious creature, loving and still wet-sinewed enough to endeavor receiving the images of another.

Or you might want to imagine one of those old-fashioned ear-trumpets, only instead of it being made of animal horn or snail shells, sheet iron or silver, imagine it rather as being "the shape of receptive listening," inviting you to venture out from the ear with your hearing in order to meet the images of the dream.

For it is this gift of our receptive listening that actually gives "body" to the image, as though the image steps through the threshold of our active hearing into substantial being. The inner ear then *becomes* the eye and we begin to actually see the images before us. So even though dream images are never more than "subtle bodies," in a very real sense we imaginally "enflesh" the image, giving it essential substance and imaginal matter with our receptive attention.

Soul-seeing is tactile. So as we begin to "see" images before us, as we touch them—that is, as we feel them—we feel them further into being. And what we discover by doing this, is that we too are touched by their being. In other words, it's our perception that brings the images further into being, but their being simultaneously brings us closer to our own. From there, it is our ongoing willingness to tend the images *as living beings*, our willingness to befriend them, to host them as though guests, that maintains them and keeps the dream alive.

This then becomes a practice for actively tuning in and turning on our inner ears, listening as though our lives depend on it. For the life of the image does indeed depend on our capacity to do this. The image itself exists as an autonomous subtle body, but the *life* of the image depends entirely upon lending our receptivity to enflesh the image's being and becoming. Without our ongoing active participation in images this way, they haven't much life beyond the initial dream; their lives, we soon discover, are through ours.

When we lend our imaginal capacities to the images in dreams we give them somewhere else to be. For what has been said here about hearing and seeing imaginally into the dream can also be said with regard to the other senses. The senses of smell, taste, and touch—all of which have corresponding organs that are located in our bodies—come together inside the heart as an organ of perception.

Working this way, we lend our imaginal bodies to the images of dreams. As we offer them our senses and our mindful attention, we develop imaginal capacities even as we work; dreamer and dream-image each informed by the other. Thus, we lend ourselves to the task of what the poet Keats called "soul-making." "I am certain of nothing," he wrote in a letter, "but the holiness of the heart's affections and the truth of imagination."

"Okay," the dreamer begins. "Well, I see an iceberg. And it's, you know, just an iceberg." She raises her hand in the air and outlines the edges of the dream iceberg, shaping it for us. "It has that classic shape that we think of when we think 'iceberg.' But the thing I notice about *this* iceberg," she continues, "is that there is a small patch of green, like a forest, on one part." She indicates a forested patch located over on the left-hand side on the imaginal iceberg. And that's it," she shrugs. "That's the whole dream."

"And where are you?" I ask.

"I'm off in space somewhere, looking at the iceberg."

"Can you see any water?"

She closes her eyes. "Yes," she answers then. "That's how I know it's an iceberg. Well, that and all the ice," she laughs.

"Notice anything else?"

"Well," she chuckles, "I remember thinking as I was dreaming, 'That's just the tip of the iceberg.'"

Everyone in the room laughs. "In other words, there's a great big part below the surface of the water that is hidden from plain view?"

"Yes," she replies.

"Anything else that you notice?"

"Well," she continues, "it's shaped exactly like Mount Hood. So it goes like this," she draws the outlined shape of Mount Hood in the air with her hands. "And it juts forward here, at Illumination Rock—the prominent, sharp-profiled summit on the upper slopes—and then it recesses back in here." She shows us.

It's happened twice now that the dreamer has outlined the shape of the iceberg with her hands; the dream, therefore, is still very much in her body.

"Like Mount Hood," I repeat back to her. Then, "What do you know about Mount Hood?"

"Well," she smiles expansively. "It's where I lived for thirty years in Oregon. It's the place that I think of whenever I think of 'home,' even though I haven't lived there for fifteen years and I know I'll never live there again." She pauses. Then quite suddenly, "Oh, look," she blurts out. "I'm crying! I never cry! And I'm crying!" She reaches for a tissue then laughs. "And here's me thinking it's a nothing dream."

I wait, allowing the importance of what's just been said to penetrate. "Are the tears related to the nostalgia of 'home'?" I ask then.

"I really loved living there," she nods.

"What did you love about it?"

"Well, I was young, for one thing," she laughs. "And I drove a truck for the Forestry Service. I sometimes drove for days on end without seeing another human being, with only flora and fauna for company. And it was heavenly." What is plain from the way she says this is that she mostly prefers the company of trees to that of humans.

"Why then did you stop?"

"It's not a place you want to be when you're old," she explains. "It's a very rugged lifestyle. I'd spend an entire day looking for wood. Then I'd collect the wood, chop the wood, split the wood, and stack the wood before carrying it into the cabin, where I'd burn the wood. Then I'd clean all the ashes from the woodstove. And the next morning, I'd wake up and have to do it all over again. I'm way too old for that now," she shakes her head.

"Okay. So the iceberg in the dream is like an iceberg version of Mount Hood, of 'home'?"

"Um-hum," she nods. "Home, only you can't go home again. As if it's frozen in time."

"Because?"

"Because you can't step in the same river twice. Because there is no 'there,' there. Because even if I went back—and I do from time to time— it's not the same. Because all that's in the past and I need to let it go."

"Well, not according to the dream."

As she turns to look at me her eyebrows knit themselves into a dark, thick scarf that slouches down over her eyes.

"You may not be able to go back home again *literally*," I say then, "to a geographical spot on the side of a mountain in Oregon—one that corresponds to coordinates on a map—but so long as you are in a body you can ever return to Mount Hood as a living image carried within the heart, as home."

"Sure," she brightens, trying, somewhat unconvincingly, to agree with me. Then, "But it's not the same, is it?"

"Oh, but it's better," I insist. "Perhaps even better than having any address on any map, anywhere." Then, "Did I ever tell you the one about the Big Pink Sea Snail?" I ask, glancing around the room. Blank faces stare back at me. "From *Doctor Dolittle?*" I add, hoping to jog their memories. But several heads now are shaking from side to side. No, it doesn't register. "Well, it goes like this," I begin.

THE BIG PINK SEA SNAIL

By the time I was twenty-one, I had moved something like twenty-seven times. For a stretch of about four or five months in the winter and spring of my nineteenth year, while going to school in Pasadena, I lived on the streets in conditions that might otherwise be called "homeless." But I have never really been homeless; for certain extended periods of time I have merely been *between houses*. And all because of the Great Pink Sea Snail in *Doctor Dolittle*.

It was Christmas Eve, 1967, and I was just about to turn six years old. As a special treat, our family went to the cinema to see Rex Harrison play Doctor Dolittle, a world-renowned veterinarian who had the unique gift of being able to speak a wide array of animal languages, all of which had been taught to him by his exotic blue macaw, Polynesia.

Well, what almost-six-year-old wouldn't adore seeing dapper Rex Harrison interact with all those exotic animals in such a sophisticated and sympathetic way?[3] He talked to the animals the way I did! Why, as far as I was concerned, it re-confirmed everything I already knew about the animal world. But it wasn't until the good Doctor Dolittle and his friends—shipwrecked on a floating island—were found by the Great Pink Sea Snail, that I was struck to the core with what, to this day, remains a central and orienting image.

From the outside, the Great Pink Sea Snail looked rather baroque and quite fantastical, like something Gaudi, the Spanish Catalonian architect, might have had a hand in creating. Nothing, however, could have prepared me for when the travelling companions of Doctor Dolittle made their way in through the aperture of the gastropod's shell and the filmmakers cut to an interior shot. For it was then that I had what is commonly referred to as a "religious experience."

The inside of that most glorious shell was nothing short of holy!— wholly big and altogether rounded with soft and inviting, oh, so feminine curves that tapered upwards in a graceful, soft-serve-like swirl. The walls of the shell were the babiest shade of pink—sparkling, iridescent, and luminous—and they were all over gently, and quite delicately, scalloped.

I don't remember many of the decorative details, though I seem
to recall curving areas piled with comfy, sleeping cushions that lined
the delicate whorls of the shell, translucent pink sheers draping down
and around that were tied back with large bows, and a little column
in the middle that, revolving around the axis of the shell, acted as a
winding staircase.

Besides all this, it was filled with everything I could imagine
might be needed or wanted in a home (except perhaps Rex Harrison).
And the Great Pink Sea Snail carried this tender, iridescent home on its
back! It was breathtakingly beautiful, fascinating, utterly inviting, and
deeply compelling.

Like Proust gone off in solemn search of his childhood madeleines,
I've thought to check these memorable impressions against the frames in
the actual film, but it seems rather beside the point. For the image as I've
carried it, or, I should say, as it's carried me since I was almost-six-years-
old, is all that really matters.

"That's it," I said aloud then, as though making some sort of
secret and sacred longing known. "I want always to be just like you,"
I whispered to the snail, as the glorious pink image sailed over the
shimmering sea of that larger-than-life screen, through the dark of that
Christmas Eve cinema, where it slid down at last and came to rest in my
young and bountiful imagination. Home.

───

"And so 'home' from that night on became wherever I am. A living image
of the snail's beautiful and abundant pink welcoming, carried within."

"So what you're saying, then, is that Mount Hood is my very own
version of your Pink Snail?" the dreamer asks.

"It can be, yes. So that if you consent to carry it as a living image in
your heart, that is, in the heart *as an organ of perception*, it can become not
only central but guiding."

"In what way can it become guiding?" another in the group asks.

"Well, for example, because I've carried this image since I was almost six, I've lived in the world as if I were 'home,' even, as I mentioned, when living on the streets in otherwise homeless conditions.

"It helps, therefore, to imagine this 'home' as a verb, rather than as a noun. For this home is not something we have; so it's rather a 'homeing,' though, of course, I just *Suessed* that word up to give you a feel for the image. Homeing is something we practice as an orientation, and as we practice this home, we simultaneously offer the ongoing sense of having a place in the world of things to others, so that they too get a sense of 'being home.'

"Homeing, then, is wherever we are, that is, wherever we are when we're moving through the world in the *imaginal ways of the heart*. So when, for example, I'm in a place that makes me feel as though I am not welcome, when I feel uncomfortable and distinctly not at home, perhaps even wary—and when it's not a case of me falling out of my own story—I can usually trust that this is due to outside forces and either I get the heck out of there, or become extremely curious about those forces that, for whatever reasons, are not interested in welcoming me, or worse, are perhaps even attempting to prevent my inner freedom. Inner freedom, of course, has everything to do with moving in the depth-filled ways of the heart."

"So how do I make what seemed to be only this morning a 'nothing' dream image and turn it into the Big Pink Sea Snail sort?" the dreamer asks then.

"Ah, such a good question. Let's see if we can answer it."

THE TROUBLE WITH IMAGES

For the Greeks, the word "soul" was an image. Yet even the word "image" makes us think of a picture or something we can see with our eyes. But "image" is much more than a visual representation of something; image, as James Hillman reminds us, refers to "the ideas that form and shape life."

But the English language is so limited; we use the word "image" for after-images—those ghost-like images that seem to almost burn into one's vision after exposure to the original image has stopped. And we also use the word for dream images, illusory images, perceptive images, and for metaphorical ideas. We talk about people and corporations in terms of the "image" that they're trying to convey, and we use the same word for false fronts and collective fantasies.

So our difficulty with the word "image" comes from the word itself, and the fact that it can be understood as either idol (as with the Greek word *eidolon*) or as icon (*eikon*).

As idol, image is experienced when we become fixed on the image itself and on our ability to see it. Then the image takes on an opacity that keeps both image and viewer trapped inside a kind of literal materiality. This renders us utterly unable to see anything beyond the image itself.

As icon, on the other hand, we see *through* the image to something that is beyond it, because what is beyond it can only be seen, that is, felt, imagined, and experienced, through it.

But it's all too easy to become confused here because we misunderstand the "mode of being" of these images, whether they are figures in our dreams or in our imaginings. We think—or perhaps "believe" is a better word—that these figures are subjectively real when we mean *imaginally* real. Or we mistakenly believe that these figures are externally real when we mean *essentially* real.

OPEN THE BOX

When I was in the second grade, our teacher instructed the students to use six specific crayon colors to draw something that we considered beautiful, something that we really, really wanted.

I worked devotedly on my drawing and was so proud of the way it turned out. I was certain that I'd be given one of those glorious golden stars that the teacher was so fond of placing on works she considered praiseworthy, those same works that she displayed at the front of the classroom. And oh, I couldn't wait to be singled out.

When the teacher handed our drawings back, however, I was completely shocked and utterly dismayed. Not only was there *not* a gold star in the upper left hand corner, there was a big red "F." Heartbroken, I was suddenly overcome with emotion.

I could barely get any words out when the teacher called me up to her desk to talk about my extravagant outburst. Slowly through my wracking tears I managed to ask her why she had given me an "F."

She said, "My dear, it's a lovely enough drawing, but you didn't follow my instructions. You were told to use six different colors. Red, pink, tan, white, blue, and yellow," she listed them. "But all I see in this drawing," she pointed, "are red, pink, and white. You didn't do as you were instructed. So, you see," she said, "that's why I gave you an 'F.'"

I was completely confused by what the teacher was saying, and at first I thought that there must be something wrong with her. For I had drawn one of those very cheesy and ridiculously frilly, heart-shaped boxes that valentine chocolates come in, using red, pink, and white crayons, just as the teacher had instructed. Oh, but that was not all.

"Did you open up the box?" I stammered, turning to the teacher. "Open up the box, and you'll see that Barbie doll I really want. She's got tan skin, yellow hair, blue eyes, and she's wearing a beautiful blue ball gown. So," I sputtered, "the box is really beautiful, the doll is something I really, really want, and I've used all six colors, just like you said."

It simply never occurred to me that the teacher would not see what I had created inside that frilly, cheesy chocolate box. For it was not just that I had imagined it—that doll was there, created by me, or perhaps together with me, and waiting to be discovered by anyone who ventured to open the lid. But slowly, excruciatingly, it began to dawn on me that what I saw, what I felt and experienced readily in the imaginal realm, others were simply not in on, or at least not in the same way that I was.

The teacher felt terrible, of course, and tried to erase the "F" by putting a cluster of gold stars on top. And she went out of her way to make a big fuss over it in front of the whole class, displaying it prominently in an attempt to make up for what had happened. But I couldn't get over it.

Looking back, it's easy to see that I had mistaken an essential image—one that was created imaginally and which existed absolutely in the imaginal realm—with something that could be readily experienced and perceived objectively, as an explicitly external image. I assumed that the Barbie was concrete and tangible, materially visible to everyone. I had no idea then, being only seven years old, that the image as it had been created through my imaginal capacities *only existed through me*, through my unique ability to perceive it *essentially*. It simply never appeared that way to me. The creeping realization that what is experienced imaginally, or not, is unique to each one of us, and that there could be as many different relationships to the imaginal realm as there are people, simply never occurred to me before.

A Nesting-Doll Place in the Family of Things

When I was about four years old, my mother went through a severe depression. Noise and light were experienced as assaults, so she kept to the dark of her bedroom with the curtains drawn for the better part of a year. During the day, my father worked and my older sister was off at kindergarten, so I was frequently shuttled off to stay with an older couple, the Kloppenburgs, out on their farm.

It was lovely to be out in the country, participating in the rhythms of the prairie with all of the farm animals, or just hanging out with Mrs. Kloppenburg. She was a very grandmotherly being who had just the right sort of knack for letting me be. She seemed to know how to let me be alongside her precisely, as a kind of gift that she gave me in an ongoing way. And oh, how I adored her. For that, and for her quiet farmer's wife strength—she was true salt of the Earth.

Days not spent at the Kloppenburg's farm were spent in our home, with my mother tucked quietly in her bed, while I was rather left to my own devices. Though my time was spent mostly alone, I do not remember being lonely at all during this time, nor do I recall that I was in any way afraid—I was probably too young yet to be afraid of most things. I also do not recall experiencing my mother's depression as something dreadful or fearful. Perhaps I took it for granted that she was experiencing something that mothers experience, for I had no way of knowing otherwise. In any case, it all seemed quite natural, as though my mother was surrendering her body to an organic healing that would eventually render her able to better navigate through life. Or not.

Now then, there was a family with five or six children living next door. I don't remember much about the family except that going over to their house—with all the noise and mess and liveliness one might expect in a family with that many children—was experienced by me as rather too chaotic, coming as I was from my own quiet little home. Because of this, I could not foray over to the neighbor's house at any one time for very long without feeling somewhat overwhelmed. But there was one thing over there that kept me going back time and again.

It was a wee box of puzzles.

Constructed of heavy-duty cardboard, there were four different puzzles in this box, each depicting a different baby farm animal in various farm settings. There was a calf, I recall, and a colt, perhaps a piglet and some ducklings, or maybe a little lamb. But what the puzzles depicted subject-wise was not at all what mattered to me. Instead, I was utterly captivated by the simple fact that individual pieces joined together to form something whole.

Not only did I sense the depth of the puzzles as wholes, I could also sense the depth of each piece wholly and separately. And I had somehow rather quickly discovered that individual constituent pieces were not interchangeable. I could not, for example, take a piece from the piglet puzzle and fit it into the calf puzzle, nor could I take a piece that belonged where the tail of the calf hung down and force it into where the ear went, though no doubt I tried.

Each piece of every puzzle had its own uniqueness, and that uniqueness belonged to a larger uniqueness, as if each piece had an individual wholeness that belonged to the particular wholeness of its puzzle, and together then those four puzzles belonged to the wholeness of the box, and the box to the toy box, and the toy box to the room, and the room to the neighbor's house, and so on, which now, with my adult imagination, can be carried all the way on out through the universe.

Though limited then to my four-year-old understanding of what the world was, it was as if each thing separately had a wholeness that was nestled inside a larger wholeness waiting to be discovered, as though the entire universe was rather like a giant nesting-doll. Seeing this, and coming into contact with it every time I was in the presence of those puzzles, filled me with great joy and wonder, and with a sense of somehow belonging to something much bigger.

And oh, how those puzzle pieces called to me, lamenting their loneliness from inside the dark of that tattered little box, otherwise crushed and forgotten about, stuffed along the side of the toy box in the far back corner of the playroom in my neighbor's messy, chaotic house.

But it was as though they knew that I could not resist their lamentations long. Soon I would make my way over to the toy box, fish the puzzle box out from among all the other well-used toys, and offer myself yet again to their pieced togetherness. Perhaps they understood, too, as I put those pieces into their waiting places to help them remember their wholeness, that I was at the very same time somehow remembering my own.

From an adult perspective, I must have looked like any young child weirdly playing with the same puzzles over and over again. But a put-together puzzle became the birthplace for images that were trying to be remembered, or *participated in*, between what was depicted, what was not depicted, and what was present and not yet present in me. In other words, the act of putting a puzzle together created a field of play between the interiority of what was depicted and the interiority of me.

When the last piece was finally fitted into place by my little hands, the depth of the depicted farm scene suddenly unfolded before my very eyes. Suddenly a sweet, spotted calf ran through a field, or a pink piglet snuffled over in the mud; a fuzzy yellow duck paddled on over-sized webbed feet in a pond, or a foal, balancing on spindly legs, looked as though it might topple over. I could smell whenever it had just rained. And the light, as it streamed through the trees and down across the landscape, was of certain sacred variety that, to this day, I still go off looking for.

I could sense the inner quality of the calf and the inner quality of the field. Even the playing itself had an inner quality. Participating in the inner quality of these things filled me with incredible delight, with love, with joy, and with the deepest kind of companioning.

And it never once occurred to me that this was in any way unique. I assumed that this kind of participatory way of being in the world was the *only* way of being in the world and that it was this way for everyone. That it was, in short, the one and only way of the world. How indeed could it have been otherwise? How could I have known any differently?

〜

The word *himma* comes to us from the Sufi tradition. It refers to the aspirating power of the heart. Through acts of meditating, conceiving, imagining, projecting, and ardently desiring, the heart's ability to think is developed and expanded to the point that it can make essentially real a being external to the person. In other words, *himma* creates as "real" the figures of the imagination, for it is the mode by which images—which we believe we've made up—appear to us as not of our making, but as genuinely created, as authentic creatures. With *himma* we come to understand these images as imaginally real, essentially real.

Without this notion of *himma*, on the other hand, we misunderstand the mode of being of these images—whether they are figures from our dreams or, as with that Barbie doll, created from the love of longing imagination. Without *himma* we fall into believing that these figures are subjectively real, that they are nothing more than an illusion, for example, or that we've created them out of some kind of fantasy, that they are our projections, or perhaps ghosts.

Without *himma* our hearts simply cannot apprehend that they are imaginatively thinking hearts. Tragically, our culture simply doesn't have an adequate psychology and philosophy of the heart, let alone one that includes the imagination. For far too long we've been told that "the mind thinks, that the heart feels, and that imagination leads us away from both."[4]

But with *himma*, love and imagination enter at the exact same moment. And it's through their equal-parts presence that we can begin to develop what Henry Corbin calls "theophanic vision," the kind of vision that, for example, perceives something other than merely a tattered bunch

of puzzles in a beaten-up and otherwise left-for-dead-box at the back of a
noisy neighbor's toy chest.

Whether waking or sleeping, images are penetrations into the worlds
they present. The task for us, then, is not to transmute dream images; the
images in dreams *come to us already invested with light*, as icons. For what
are dreams but inner illuminations? Those dreams that are entrusted to
our care, the ones that we remember and that commonly arrive in the
dead of night, in the dark of sleep, when we are tucked up in our little
beds with our eyes closed, as various and sundry images step forth from
the discreet shadows to reveal themselves as beings of light.

Now whether these beings of light come as part of the *dramatis
personae,* or as props, or as the part of the setting, or perhaps as nothing
more than simply a mood, matters far less than the fact that the
images come at all. Yet the moment we awaken we forget this. And we
immediately set about eying the dream with fixed and narrow waking-
world ideas that darken, dull, and divest the inherent light from the
images, indeed from the dream, which in turn divests the light from the
dream of life itself.

This then is our task: to transmute our vision so that dream images
remain in the same light-invested manner in which they are created and
first received by us. By doing this we begin to understand that dreaming
is not something we do. Rather, dreaming is happening all the time (as
many tribal peoples already know). The aboriginal people of Australia,
for example, have a marvelous expression for this: *yaro yaro,* which means
"everything dreaming all the time." Thus, by transforming our vision
we begin to see through the surface of things to the light from which all
things have emerged.

Culturally, however, we suffer from a kind of imaginal atherosclerosis. As fatty material thickens and hardens forming calcium deposits that collect along the walls of our arteries, blocking access to our hearts, so too our vision has become blocked and cut off, fixated merely on the fatty surface of things.

The current debate among researchers about where precisely dreams originate in the brain—in the way-back brain stem or in the forebrain— illustrates vision that is fixed on the scientific surface of things. Maybe dreams originate in the brain stem, or in the forebrain, or maybe they don't. From an imaginal perspective it doesn't much matter; the brain (though not the brain alone, isolated from being) certainly allows us to recognize, vividly participate in, and later recall *something that is going on in the realm of the heart all the time.*

ECHIDNA DREAMING

Not long ago I had to visit to my dentist for a root canal. While waiting for the numbing to take effect, the doctor asked what I do "for a crumb." Upon hearing that I work with dreams, he made some comment about how he never dreams.

"Actually," I said, "scientists tell us that all mammals—and birds, for that matter—dream, and that, on average, human beings dream for about two hours every night."

"All mammals and birds, eh?"

"Well, they're actually having difficulty proving this for the echidna," I said. "But that's because they're looking in all the wrong places."

"*The echidna?*" He turned to look at me, his face a question mark. "That curious, egg-laying creature from Australia?"

I nodded. "Researchers have spent a good deal of time looking to cycles of REM sleep for evidence that we dream," I continued. "Human beings, for example, have four to five rapid eye movement cycles per night on average. And if a human is awakened after one of these cycles, they can most usually, that is, eighty to ninety-five percent of the time, vividly recall their dreams. If awakened during other stages of sleep, however, humans seem able to recall their dreams only about ten percent of the time.

"In humans, the first REM cycle lasts about fifteen minutes, the second for about twenty minutes, and so forth. The length of dreams—it was discovered when researchers awakened dreamers after a cycle of REM sleep—precisely corresponds to the length of that REM cycle."

"But not for the echidna?"

"Well, so far scientists have been unable to prove that the echidna *has* REM sleep. Therefore researchers lean toward also concluding that the echidna does not dream."

"Hmh."

"But what scientists are actually measuring, at least, near as I can tell, is not dreaming at all but rather *dreaming recall*. It seems that it is the ability to remember dream images during REM sleep that is increased, not dreaming itself."

"Hmmhh," the dentist articulated again, only slightly louder this time. Then, "How's the numbing coming along?" he asked, peering intently at my mouth.

"Not quite there," I answered, pressing my fingers along my lower lip. Then, "The neurons that course through our brains during REM sleep fire like mad. They are more active during REM sleep than they are at any other time, including even our most motivated waking states. What floods our brains is a biologically ancient chemical called 'acetylcholine.' And its function, bizarrely enough, is wakefulness; it works to focus our attention vividly. So from the biochemistry involved, it's like REM sleep provides the perfect conditions for us to learn."

"Very curious," said the good doctor, snapping on his purple, grape-scented latex gloves.

"Even more curious," I went on, "is that acetylcholine is what's missing in folks who suffer from Alzheimer's." But by this point I was beginning to slur my words; the tip of my tongue and my lower lip were numb enough to begin. I therefore stopped my dream speech and let the doctor and his assistant get on with their work.

At some point into the procedure, however, I nodded off. A moment or two later I awoke with a start, which in turn startled the poor dentist (who'd been peering into my mouth with one of those overhead microscopes, while gently probing the lengths of my root canals with one of his delicate measuring instruments) and his assistant (whose water-squirting gizmo went flying, spewing cold water all over my face and neck). I sputtered an open mouth apology then as the assistant laughed and mopped up my face. Fumbling for his equipment, the dentist chuckled, "Well, too bad your little nap wasn't long enough for you to dream," he said, placing his eyes against the microscope as he settled back into a more comfortable excavating position.

Ah, but the whole point of telling this story is to highlight the fact that in those few moments of nodding off, all sorts of images did indeed present themselves to me, as if in a dream. The "packaging" or "wrapping" we generally expect our dreams to be in was not present. In other words, there wasn't a dreaming "I" at the center of any kind of narrative or plot. And the ability to recall the content of the images was also absent. But the point is, that there were several images that indeed stepped forth and announced themselves before finally fading away as I woke up.

What this suggests (again!) is that dreaming is not something we "do." Rather, dreaming, or the images present in what we commonly call our dreams, is an ongoing activity that, for the most part, remains below

the threshold of waking consciousness. When we fall asleep, however—
and especially during cycles of REM sleep, as well as during those in-
between, threshold times when we are either just falling asleep or waking
up—we are rendered able to notice and remember this ongoing activity
more vividly.

But why does it matter that dreaming is an ongoing activity rather
than something we do? Because if we can begin to understand dreaming,
or what we think of as dreaming, as the soul's own mode of activity, we
can gradually allow ourselves to be shaped by it.

⚍

"Well okay, but how do we do that?" asks the Mount Hood dreamer. "I
mean, precisely. How do I begin to 'see' this iceberg image as home?"

"Well, you'd start by looking 'through' it, *with* it, rather than 'at' it.
The mistake we commonly make has to do with abstracting away from
the dream images to look for meaning. But this would be to look 'at'
the dream images. So if you leave here this evening with the notion that
whenever you dream of Mount Hood, or of an iceberg for that matter, it
'means' home, I will have done you a great disservice. This is my ongoing
critique of so-called symbol work, where symbols have been reduced
from images that are alive, that is, *as beings*, into what they 'mean' to us."

What Does Fox Mean?

To illustrate, a woman comes to me with a dream of a fox. "Yesterday,"
she begins, "I dreamt that I was walking down the street with my
husband, and there—just sitting on the corner—was a fox." She looks at
me with an air of expectancy. "What does *fox* mean?" she asks then.

But when I ask her why she doesn't want to know what her husband
means, she laughs, dismissing the question—for she assumes that what

she knows about her husband in the waking-world is also true of him in her dream. She is not interested, therefore, in the "meaning" of her husband in the dream any more than she is interested in the meaning of him in the waking-world.

Yet the dreamer forgets one very important thing: that the image in her dream is not literally her husband—for he is, as one might assume, beside her in bed, sleeping and dreaming just as is she. Indeed, it is not until her husband does something in a dream that disturbs the woman that she might ask, "What does it *mean* that he was doing that?"

<hr>

"Like this woman, most of us have been conditioned to ask: 'What does this mean?' This question, however, as Steve Aizenstat reminds us, 'tends to freeze the dream within one of a multitude of intricately contrived psychological systems,' even as it ignores the simple truth that dreaming reality is just as real as those trees outside. Or as that lamp over there, on the desk."

"But there's no such thing, *really*, as a Mount Hood iceberg," the dreamer says, corkscrewing her head to eye me sideways.

"But isn't it the Mount Hood iceberg that, as you outline its shape for us, touches you so deeply that you shed real tears?"

"Yes," she concedes. "But not when I originally dreamt it," she adds quickly.

"And yet, isn't it as though the 'shape' of that iceberg is reaching through the depths of your slumber to touch you still, even now, that your heart might be opened just enough to allow something between you and the Mount Hood iceberg image to unfold?"

She shrugs. But what's evident then is her desire to fall into this idea, yet it's as if all of her accumulated experience struggles to keep the upper hand.

Oh, from where does all of this resistance come? And why is it so hard for us moderns to imagine that we are loved?

"Well," the Mount Hood Iceberg dreamer says, "I'd like to believe that, but my inner skeptic is at the same time saying that perhaps the iceberg is nothing more than a reaction to the peppermint patty that I ate before going to bed."

"And it might be," I laugh. "But which is the better story? Given a choice between a loving, ongoing relationship that is trying to take root in the home of your heart, and a digestive reaction, which will you choose?" Then, before she can answer, "But now remember I'm a mythologist. Mythologists collect stories—we don't feel compelled to choose a winner."

"So it's a trick question?"

"There's room enough for both stories," I chuckle. "Indeed, there's room for many, many stories. So the dream can be about something imaginally trying to take root in your heart as an organ of perception *and* trying to digest some late-night, chocolate, minty thing at the same time. The more you hold this one wee image, the more you will begin to see all that emerges from it."

"And they can all be true?" another in the room asks.

"Absolutely. Yes. For this is one way that dreams love us—our engagement with images is what encourages this kind of continual revelation. And the more we engage with them, the more they reveal themselves through us. It's a kind of a *quid pro quo* exchange that is always, *always* asking to be made. But we are required, indeed needed, in order that the depths of the images are revealed at all, *even to the images themselves*."

"Well, it helps that you believe in dreams," someone else says then.

"Actually, they don't really require that we believe in them. But yes, I do believe that Psyche isn't out to get us. I have psychological

faith that as images, as souls, we are indeed aimed at a certain star. And
that for each one of us it's different depending on what we came here to
remember and display. It doesn't have to be true in a capital 'T' kind of
way, it merely has to be true enough—a good story that brings us to the
truth of things as they are essentially."

Then, "What might it be like," I press the dreamer gently, "if you
were to allow that unfolding in an ongoing way? If you were to keep
dreaming the shape of the Mount Hood iceberg with your hands each
morning until, like Harold with his purple crayon," I raise my hand to
demonstrate, "it becomes a portal to the actual place, to home?"

"Harold? Who's Harold?" someone asks then, like "Did I
miss something?"

"From *Harold and the Purple Crayon*," I answer, looking around the
room. From the expressions on their faces, however, it's clear that no one
has read the book. "It's a children's story about the imaginal realm," I
explain. "One night Harold wanted to go for a walk in the moonlight,"
I say, recounting how the story opens, "but since there wasn't a moon,
Harold pulled out his purple crayon and drew one up in the night sky.
And there was also no path, so he used his crayon and drew a path . . . "[5]
And on and on it goes, as the dramatic and ever enchanting adventures of
Harold and his purple crayon begins. Oh, it's a delightful book. And it's
all right there, in the pages of that children's story. You need never read
another book."

"He creates a world just by drawing it?"

"An imaginal world. And then he enters it. And it's just like that for
you, only using your hand instead of a purple crayon."

"Just by believing in it?" the dreamer asks. "So like Dorothy in the
Wizard of Oz saying, 'There's no place like home. There's no place like
home,' over and over until *poof!* she finds herself there?"

"There is a ritual, incantational aspect to it, yes," I answer. "But it's more than 'believing' in the image that produces the effect. It also has everything to do with giving yourself over to it, that is, surrendering to the longing and desire of it."

"Oh," she says simply. "I knew there was a catch."

"In other words, if you really want to go home you will first be required to give up this notion that you can't. You'll need to surrender the idea that home is somewhere you left fifteen years ago and that it's gone forever."

She takes a deep, sounding breath.

"And then you have to go after the image with your whole heart— ardently desiring *home*. Indeed, you'll become 'longing for home' bodily, as if on a cellular level, until you finally have 'home' in your sights, a mere hand's length away," I raise my hand to draw the outline of the iceberg again, carefully. "One . . . last . . . outline . . ."

Then, "Oh, but here comes the hardest part . . . because it's then that you'll need to surrender this idea of ever 'having' home, and instead allow the image to enter you, bodily. That is, if it so chooses. For we can never force our desires on the imaginal realm, it's always, *always* a matter of grace. All we can ever do is create the right conditions wherein the imaginal realm simply cannot resist us."

There is a kind of silence that overtakes the room then, which is less like an absence of noise and more like a gathering of . . . what? Of courage? Of love? Of a willingness to try? Slowly and quite deliberately, the dreamer raises her right hand and begins outlining the Mount Hood iceberg again. Almost immediately the image shows itself.

"Ummm," the dreamer sighs, as some of the tenderness that's been looking for her finds her at last. And we are all of us touched then through the tenderness that is between them.

"Images are penetrations into the worlds they're in," I continue quietly, allowing the image and the dreamer to stay in their tender embrace. "But they are also always trying to penetrate us. Perhaps they are trying to help us to remember that we, too, are beings of light?"

Then, "What, if anything, do you notice about the image now?" I ask, after a time.

"Well," she answers in a voice that seems to come from down around her knees, "instead of having a few glaciers, like Mount Hood, it's solid ice, except for that weird little out-of-place patch of green, and almost the whole thing is submerged under water."

"What makes that patch of green 'weird'?" the woman next to her asks.

"Well, what's it doing on an iceberg?" she laughs.

"Did you find it weird as you were dreaming, when you awoke and reflected on the dream, or just now?"

She takes a moment to think about this. "I thought it was weird as I dreamt. I'm like, 'What's that doing there?' And weird, too, or rather still, when I awoke. But it's that weirdness, I think, that helped me to remember the dream at all."

"Because it struck you as so peculiar?"

"Um-hum," she nods.

"James Hillman tells us that 'soul is most profoundly moved by images that are distorted, unnatural, twisted, and in pain.' So you're absolutely right—it's likely that the peculiarity of the little green patch did indeed help you to remember the dream. Let's get curious about that green patch," I suggest then. "What sort of green is there in that patch?"

"Trees."

"Tropical trees?"

"No," she says in such a way as to suggest that there is really only one kind of trees. "Like those that are found in the Pacific Northwest," she says. "Conifers," she adds, in case I don't know. "It's so green and wet and lush in the rainforest there—they get one hundred and twenty inches of rain annually—that you cannot see the fauna. Animals are in abundance but the forest is simply too dense, too lush, to see them. A deer, for example, can be a alongside the road and you'd never see it from your vehicle."

"And that's what the little patch of green on this iceberg is like?"

She nods and repeats, "lush," in such a lush voice that Rumi walks into the room.

"Ah, our old friend and mentor, Rumi, has just walked into the room," I say, reaching for the well-worn book of poetry waiting with tail-wagging eagerness next to me on a shelf. "Ah, yes," the poem finds me almost immediately. "It's just this one stanza from 'The Dream That Must Be Interpreted.' It goes like this:

> We began
> as a mineral. We emerged into plant life
> and into the animal state, and then into being human,
> and always we have forgotten our former states,
> except in early spring when we slightly recall
> being green again.[6]

"'When we slightly recall being green again.' Isn't that what we respond to each Spring? The 'darling buds of May,' as Shakespeare puts it. For, as they say, 'hope springs eternal'—but isn't this because Spring springs eternal? Spring gives us hope for life after life, after death, and for love after love, for the ever-greening possibilities of nature—*our* nature, and the world's. So perhaps the 'weird' patch of green on the iceberg of the dream is like this love after love that is trying to ever orient us to the imaginal possibilities of our nature, which, of course, is precisely how Carl Jung defines the soul."

We have a tendency to think of soul as something we possess. Jung, however, defined the soul quite simply as "the imaginative possibilities of our nature." What's so appealing about his minimalist definition is that it doesn't try to tell us what soul is. It suggests rather that we give our attention to a particular kind of inner activity—as the "spontaneous, ever-present, coming into being and passing away of images."[7] What this further suggests is that it's best to approach soul by way of characterizing, that is, by showing how soul functions, rather than by definition.

So rather than trying to give attention to soul, the knack is to render oneself ever more capable of, and more receptive to, images—as ideas that shape and form life—for the sake of the images themselves. If we can understand the image *as an activity of the soul*, regardless of its content, we can begin to develop capacities for becoming increasingly aware of soul life in an ongoing way.

Thus, it's important not to become too distracted by the contents of images. So the practice is to get a sense of the dream's movement—its rhythms, its ups and downs, lefts and rights, ins and outs, and so forth— the dramatic action of the imaging process itself.

Any meaning that can be wrought from the dreamtime, therefore, has much more to do with coming to sense the soul as an activity, in other words, as a relationship between the dreamer and the imaginative possibilities of his or her nature, than it has to do with what an image "means."

The attention-grabbing green patch, then, has everything to do with the evergreen forests of possibility in all of us. And it is the remembrance of this ever-greening, attention-grabbing possibility that becomes a kind of homecoming, a return to soul and to who we are really. So when folks talk about a return to the Garden of Eden, it's not a return to a geographical place, to a garden that can be found on a map; it's an ongoing orientation to being.

Which returns us now to the question of how to begin to "see" through the iceberg image to "home"—as an orientation to being— and to see through the lush forest to be reminded of our ever-greening possibilities. We need be reminded to "stick with the image," but we also want to devote ourselves to the task of transmuting our vision, so that the images might remain in the same light-invested manner in which they are originally received by us.

We have a tendency to archive the dream as a kind of static image, rather like a photograph, or a DVD. And then we file them away in our dream cabinet. This one goes under "kinky sex" and this one under "animal." But dreams are alive; images are alive. And it's perhaps only our lust for understanding—which is more often than not merely code for "having dominion over" the dream—that would reduce it to its so-called meaning.

Ego wants dominion over the dream (in the same way that it wants dominion over everything). It wants to file this dream here and that dream there and be done with it. If everything has a place in the ego-driven, dream-cabinet fantasy of ours, then we can blithely continue to pride ourselves into believing that we know ourselves. But, of course, we do not. We are not merely the products of our upbringing, or of our genetic endowment, or of some combination of these. And we are not merely what we appear to be. Nor are we what it *feels* like to be us on the inside. We are what we can be, but what we can be is being given to us dream by dream, moment by moment, image by image.

≈

"I think I can see how the green patch of the iceberg dream might lend itself to ongoing possibilities for the kind of greening that you're talking about," another woman in the dream group says. "But what if the image that sticks around is not so pleasant. What if there's nothing 'green' about it? What if it's downright . . ." she trails off, looking for just the right word.

"The same thing applies. It would be a mistake to take the kind of greening that we've been talking about literally," I answer, but the dreamer's expression conveys her general disbelief.

"Look," I say then. "There are several things that dreams are simultaneously trying always to do. There is no way to convey these simultaneous activities of the dreamtime, however, except to list them individually. But this runs the risk that we might fall into a kind of 'mentaling' of the dream. In other words, we could easily fall into thinking 'about' the dream rather that 'with' it. So it's important to keep coming back to the imaginal language of dreams.

"It's likewise important to bear in mind that when patients made their way to Aesculapian temples looking for a cure, the visit that the god paid to them during their sleep wasn't made in order to give folks something to do, something to obtain or pursue in the waking-world in order that they might be cured. *The dream itself was the cure.*

"So what we do with the dream in waking life, if anything," I continue, "needs to be a careful extension of the dream itself. Therefore we want to cultivate waking-world practices that share a close affinity, 'a sympathy of being,' as the Sufis say, with the spontaneous activity of dreaming.

"To that end, let's see if we can't discover what dreams are trying to do by working with the not-so-pleasant dream you have in mind, the dream that, as you say, is decidedly not green," I suggest.

Immediately, however, there is a good deal of resistance present in the dreamer, and it becomes apparent that she does not want to share her dream. Several others in the group remind her that by talking about the dream as we have in general terms, the dream is already asking to be in the room. "If we leave here tonight with these images still locked inside of

you," the woman sitting next to the reluctant one says, "not only will we
not hear into the images for *their* sake, but my guess is that you will leave
here thinking that this is a dream about you."

The dreamer mulls this over. Then slowly, hesitantly, she begins to
tell the dream. "I am in a public place," she says. "I have no idea where
exactly. But almost immediately I need to go to the bathroom. At the
doorway to the bathroom I am filled with a kind of dread, which is not
unlike the kind of dread I experience in the waking-world regarding
public bathrooms. I turn the light on to discover that there are only two
stalls. I pick the first stall and enter. Then, just as I am sitting down on
the toilet, the door—which I could have sworn I locked—slowly starts
to creak open. I immediately begin kicking and punching and shoving
defensively, as if to save my life from what's on the other side of the door,
even though I cannot see anything.

"But what I feel when I punch and kick and shove—though, like I
say, I cannot see anything—is that the thing on the other side is some sort
of being, a creature that is soft, that is, *not rigid*, and quite definitely alive.
In other words, whatever is on the other side is not a thing; it's a being of
some sort. I kick violently at the creature, giving it everything I've got,
when suddenly I hear that it's whimpering," she gasps then to display her
shock, her horror and dismay. "I immediately stop kicking and punching
and I am filled with a kind of . . ." she pauses as the emotion begins to take
her, bodily, from the ground up, "regret and remorse . . ." she manages to
say, before being overtaken completely.

<hr>

It's important to recognize that the emotion that suddenly engulfs the
dreamer is merely another image of the dream. As such, we want to give
it enough freedom to move around the room with those more visually
"pictorial" images that have now been given a kind of "shore leave" by

the dreamer. At the same time, however, we don't want to lose sight
of the wholeness of the dream. In the presence of strong emotion, we
become more the objects of attention than people capable of attending to
others (let alone to the images in our dreams).

Yet if we can come to the point of realizing that dream images,
in effect, draw emotions out from deep within our soul life for us to
experience directly *because they want something from us*, we can begin to
recognize the autonomy of both dream images and of emotions. When
we can do this with emotion, the emotion no longer has us so tightly in its
grip. And this frees us up enough to get curious about what the emotion
might want from us. The trick is to get ever curiouser.

The task, therefore, is neither to hold emotions back, nor to let them
run away with us, but rather to get a kind of participatory look at them
through the wholeness of the dream, that is, in the context of the other
images. Emotion, however strongly experienced, is but *one* of the images
asking for our mindful attention in dreams. If we miss this, we miss what
dreams are trying to teach us, which has less to do with the content of
dream images and their so-called ability to bring ever more consciousness
for living, and more to do with how to be present to and for the activity of
soul. As the "spontaneous, ever-present, coming into being and passing
away of images," and in the face of strong and increasingly stronger
emotions, dreams endeavor to teach us presence.

As an aside, it's important to keep the dream in the present tense. So
that instead of saying, as for example with this dream, "I *was* in a public
place," the dreamer says, "I *am* in a public place." This helps to keep us
from falling into an "archival" stance with the dream. It allows the dream
to be alive in the "now of nows," as Stella Adler used to say. The dream,
in other words, is dreaming right now. This not only encourages the

images to be present with us right now in the room in an unfolding sort of way, it also invites us to be present to and for the images right now in the room in an unfolding sort of way. This minor realignment to the present tense brings with it major possibilities for learning the kind of presence that dreams are always trying to teach.

—

As the "divine influx" of emotion mingles with the other dream images, the whimpering creature dream is repeated back to the dreamer, keeping the dream in the present tense. This adds even more body to the dream images. As this takes place, the dreamer is invited to notice what she notices in a "just so" kind of way, that is, phenomenologically, and to let the rest of us in on it. This is how we open up the dream, giving the images more body and ever more freedom to move around the room.

This encourages the images, encourages the dream, and even encourages the dreamer. The Irish philosopher George Berkeley once said that "to be, is to be perceived." Our perception of the images, our capacity to see into them, to hear into, touch into, taste and smell into images is what reveals them to us and, as it turns out, to the images themselves.

At the same time, you may have noticed that the Mount Hood Iceberg dream, though still in the room, has stepped back into the more discreet shadows along the edges out of a kind of courtesy, in order to give these newly introduced dream images enough leg room, that is, enough space, to be perceived. It is only when an image does *not* exhibit this kind of courtesy with other images that we come to understand that it has not been given the proper kind of attention by us. And so we come at it again, hearts and senses wide open, bowing before what it might yet want from us.

JEREMY DREAMING

Once upon a time, a woman called and asked me to tend a dream with her. Even in the silence that gathered before she said hello and introduced herself, however, what was entirely clear to me was that this young woman's hair was on fire. In other words, she didn't have the dream—the dream had her. Turns out, she hadn't slept well in several years and that when she was able to fall asleep at all, dreams disturbed her sleep very, very much. From her perspective, dreams were making things far worse for her in the waking-world, not better.

In the particular dream that prompts her to call, she is in underworld caverns that remind her of the catacombs of Paris, walking with a small group of people who she seems to know from the dreamtime. Suddenly a figure steps forth from the shadows of the catacombs. It is someone she recognizes from the waking-world, an old boyfriend named Jeremy, who is no longer in the land of the "living living," as they say.

"He looks lost and confused, and sort of like a zombie," the young woman says. "Like he's been walking around down there for years, since he died, in a state of utter confusion. And he's walking the other way. I mean he's walking in the opposite direction that the rest of us are headed. So I go over to him and say, 'Jeremy, come with us. Come walk with us.' But he looks at me and doesn't even seem to recognize me. He just looks lost and confused. He looks at me so intently then, as if he is trying to remember who I am, that, for a second there, I think he will remember me. 'It's me,' I say, and I am frantically trying to get him to remember me.

"I want to touch him but for some reason physically touching him is not an option. It's somehow out of the question. And yet I can't imagine how he does not recognize me. And I think, 'If only I could touch him he would remember me,' but I cannot. I am imploring him to remember me with my eyes, my words, my longing. He looks at me for a second

or two more, then, still dazed and confused, he moves on in the same
direction that he was headed in earlier. Soon, he is disappeared again into
the dark of the catacombs and I am left with no choice but to go back with
the others and to continue walking in the opposite direction with them.
I wake up sobbing and terrified, knowing that Jeremy wants something
from me but I don't know what."

It is subsequently revealed to me by the dreamer that Jeremy was
killed in sudden, unexpected, and entirely brutal circumstances. Several
years earlier, while attending an all-night "zombie rave" that he'd
organized for a bunch of kids in their late teens and early twenties, a
homeless man who had also been at the party left for a brief time and
then returned. Upon his return, he pulled out a shotgun and opened fire,
killing seven people, including himself; Jeremy was one of the victims.

So distraught was this young woman when we tended the dream
together that I became caught in trying to comfort her. She was supposed
to have been at the party that night, but at the last moment she changed
her mind, deciding not to attend.

I did not know just how much I had "wronged" the dream, however,
until later, after our session was over, and I was back up at my house. I
walked into the kitchen to put my dirty teacup into the sink and when
I turned around, the image of Jeremy was standing right there in the
middle of my kitchen.

"Oh," I said, startled to see him. He didn't say or gesture anything.
He didn't need to; I knew immediately that what I had done in trying
to comfort the young woman was wrong, offensive to the dream, and to
Jeremy Dreaming.

Then, oh, so tenderly, "Hello, Jeremy. You're up here where
you don't belong for a reason. I am so sorry. I see by your being
here, however, that you have forgiven me and that you are asking for
something more, perhaps for a different kind of attention? Come along.

We'll take you back down to my office and tend to you there," I said. And slowly, carefully, I made my way back down the slow zig-zagging steps to my office at the bottom of the hill.

I lit a candle and immediately called the young woman back. I apologized and proceeded to explain what had just happened with the dream image of Jeremy. But I think I must have spooked the hell out of her. I had hoped that she would continue to work with me for the sake of Jeremy Dreaming, but it was not to be.

There in my office, however, I stayed and tended to the dream. This image, like so many others that have been entrusted to my care, is one I tend in an ongoing way. For dream images not only touch us, they befriend our existence in such a way that with us, through us, they indeed exist.

DREAMS AS AFTERLIFE

Because the "dead" so often visit the living in dreams, questions regarding the possibility of an afterlife are quite commonly asked. Based on the many, many dreams that involve the deceased—in what, if we were still living tribally, might be considered "visitations"—there is ample anecdotal "evidence" to support the idea of life after death.

Dreams in which the dead appear, however, might also express our attempts to deal with our feelings toward those who have died, or perhaps our own feelings about death in general.

When someone near to us dies we go through a period of adjustment. No longer able to relate to them in their physical presence, it is perhaps their physical absence that—if we are but willing to surrender our longing and desire—prompts the move into their imaginal presence.

But what if our dreams are the afterlife? Or if not *the* afterlife, what if our dreams are an other-than-this-life for the deceased? If we can at least open ourselves to this idea in an imaginal way, then what we make of our dreams, how we make ourselves present to them and for them matters perhaps a whole lot more than we generally care to consider. Taken further, our dreams matter not merely in terms of ourselves alone, in terms of our stories and "what does this mean to me?" but also for the sake of those who have gone before us, for the dearly departed.

It's excruciatingly hard, however, to be in conscious connection with one who has died, because our unconscious desires are working at full speed. So a lot of inner work has to be done to really have the experience that one who has died now lives according to different "laws," that they are indeed beings of light. If we approach them in order to satisfy our grief, our longings, and our desires, such an approach fetters their soul/spirit being to want to return. This can excite the deceased's desires—which they are in the midst of letting go of—thereby running the risk that they might lose direction and want to be back here with us in a physical, embodied way.

So the task for us here on this side involves learning to move into our grief as a way of holding the memories of those who have died, so that they too might begin to adjust to being in the imaginal realms. To do this, of course, we need to let the literal go. Only then we can begin to discover that there is another dimension to grief.

If we can allow ourselves to be with the memories of those who have died—those memories that are theirs and not merely ours, we can gradually begin to be with the departed as imaginal presences rather than as things to cry about. Moving into relationship with those who have died *as images*, as beings of dreaming light, gives them another place to be, in other words, an afterlife as imaginal presences.

———

"Does that mean that the . . ." one of the dreamers begins, then pauses, "well, that the spirit of Jeremy, or the ghost of him or whatever, lives here in your office?" Her voice goes up almost an entire octave by the end of her question.

"Yes and no," I smile. "Jeremy Dreaming lives here, but not the ghost of him. I don't know enough about ghosts to offer anything other than they are reported as visiting most frequently during liminal space, especially during that threshold time when we are in the midst of falling asleep, in the same time, for example, that we experience that strange bodily sensation of tripping or falling down stairs.

"And yes, Jeremy Dreaming lives here, but he does not *only* live here. In other words, the particular image that was created between the dreamer, the dream, and me, that is, through my particular attention and imaginal perception, well, *that* image does indeed live here.

"But my good guess is that the original dream image lives on in the tormented, sleepless nights of the dreamer as well. And we can only wonder how many other Jeremy Dreaming images have made different visitations to others, perhaps to those in his family, or his friends, or to the people in his 'clan.' (Who are all those people in the dreamtime who seem to know us so intimately anyway?)

"But all of those Jeremy Dreaming images have not been entrusted to my care. *This* Jeremy Dreaming, however, has, and so it's toward this image that I turn my heart and my imaginal attention."

"But are they same?" she asks. "I mean, not the same but . . ." she trails off, not knowing quite how to word her question.

"It's likewise for all of us," I say. "Let's take you, for example. My guess is that you're different depending who you're with. You are one version—or perhaps 'reflection' is a better word—of you with your daughter, for example. And another when you're with your best friend. And still another when you're with your husband, your father, your sisters, your aunts, your clients. Virtually everyone. For we are who we are *always* in relation to another, or in relation to a particular place, or a piece of art, or, or, or . . . the list goes on and on. We are beings in context.

"Now some of these versions, or reflections, of you can be quite similar, only subtly different, nuanced, or they can be remarkably different. But you're never not you, right? Except in those moments when you might become possessed by an emotion like rage or something. And then no one recognizes you; *you* don't even recognize you! You're left shaking your head and wondering, 'What the hell was *that?*'"

"Oh, that's so true," she says then, as if this has never before occurred to her.

"So who we are has a good deal to do with how we are received," I continue. "Well, it's no different with dream images. They are who they can be around us. And because the dream is happening now in the active space being created in an ongoing way, that is, between us, the dream that unfolds is not the exact dream that the dreamer dreamt. So, for example, in the dream we're working with, the public bathroom looks and feels a certain way to the dreamer, and it might look and feel quite different to me, and quite different again to every one of you. But like different versions of the same myth, all versions are true and correct so long as they are essentially true and correct to the image itself, to the dream.

"We are not interested in photocopying the dream then handing it around for everyone to look at as though it were 'exhibit A.' What we are interested in is the dream's unfolding, but this will be different for each one of us depending on the capacities of our imaginal instruments, different for each one of us depending on our hearts as organs of perception.

"So just as the Sufis say that 'each of us gets the God we are capable of,' it is likewise with dream images. In other words, each of us gets the dream we are capable of—even if the dreams we are working with when we work in a group this way, are not dreamt by us, that is, by us individually. The task, therefore, is to make ourselves ever more capable of receiving images on their terms. And one can only get a feel for this by doing it; it's a practice that develops the heart as an organ of perception over time.

"So the Jeremy Dreaming that lives here is different than the Jeremy Dreaming that hangs around with the young woman from Portland who called me," I continue. "For one thing, he and I have no history together. So the lack of personal history between us frees him from any desire of who I want or need him to be."

"Well, what *does* he want?" she asks.

"With me?"

She nods.

"To be."

"That's it?" she asks. "That's all?"

"That's everything. To be allowed to be in an ongoing way, precisely. In other words, uniquely." Then, "But the whole reason for telling this story is to highlight for you that the Mount Hood Iceberg dream has indeed stepped back out of courtesy—in a way that Jeremy Dreaming did not when I first attempted to tend that dream. The Mount Hood Iceberg dream, on the other hand, has stepped back in order to give the bathroom creature dream more of the careful attention it seeks. So settle in and get your dark feelers on."

﹦

"When I hear the dream back," the dreamer says after a time, her eyes welling up, "I am filled with tremendous sadness. The same sadness that's been with me since the dream first presented itself to me. It's the whimpering, the vulnerability of the creature on the other side, that makes me so sad. When I hear that—and I can hear it still—I am plunged into darkness and confusion. I am completely undone by that whimpering."

"Yes, there is something so very tenderizing in hearing the sound of that creature's vulnerability," I agree. "But isn't this why the creature is in the dream in the first place?"

The dreamer tilts her head to look at me as her eyes narrow into slots only slightly thicker than a dime.

"To evoke this kind of tenderizing?"

She shrugs.

"Doesn't its vulnerability open your own? Remember, the dreamtime places us next to the River of Dreams where and when we are able to cross. Precisely. In other words, we get the kinds of dreams that undo us when we *can*, when we are psychically and spiritually robust enough to be undone. 'For the status of personhood is not given; it must be won.' It's our undoing, and the presence of sadness of this sort, of darkness and confusion, as you put it, brought on by the penetrating sound of the whimpering creature, that moves us into Mystical Poverty."

Mystical Poverty is a term brought to us by the 17th century Shi'ite mystic Mir Damad. It refers to "the great occult clamor of beings," the "silent clamor of their metaphysical distress," that appeared to him as "a music of cosmic anguish along with a sudden black light that invaded the entire universe."[8] The true state of all beings, says Mir Damad, is that everything in creation *has* nothing in itself and indeed *is* nothing in itself.

Mir Damad's dream reveals that each of us is a twofold being. The lit up, illuminated being—experienced rather readily in the waking-world and likewise in dreams as the "dreaming-I"—is that being that convinces us that we know ourselves. But we do not. For there is another side to being—the black-light side—which is the side the mystic perceives. And this side reveals our "poverty," for it shows us the side of being that we do not know. The totality of being means, therefore, that we are creatures that we both know and don't know at the same time.

It is through Mystical Poverty, that is, through the enduring and unbreakable unity of these two beings in creation, that we can begin to perceive the beauty, the animation, and the personification of all the things of this world. Thus, it is by our ongoing willingness to surrender what we know, or what we think we know, to what we do not, to what we might never know, that, as Tom Cheetham reminds us, "our certainties, our graspiness, and our hardnessess of heart can be undone."

For our bathroom-creature dreamer this takes the form of a shattering experience, undoing all the solid foundations upon which the ego and its literal world are built. For Mystical Poverty reveals that each of us can only be as we are made-to-be, and that we are limited to this and by this. This then is another one of those simultaneous things that the dreamtime is always endeavoring—to penetrate us enough to move us into a conscious, ongoing awareness of, and relationship to, our Mystical Poverty.

"What if the dream doesn't evoke this kind of opening sadness? What if it's just *gruesome?* Horrifying and . . ." another dreamer suddenly pipes up, "sick. I mean I heard what you said about the soul being profoundly moved, you know, like what Hillman says, but why does it have to be so very twisted? Why does it have to be *so* gruesome?"

"How long has this particular gruesome dream image hung around?"

"A week," she shrugs. "Maybe a bit longer. But I have a lot of gruesome dreams. I mean, all the time, all the time, gruesome."

"And that causes you to imagine that you are . . . ?"

"Gruesome," she says, sucking in air as she says this, while running her fingers through her hair. "That there's something wrong with me.

I'm not getting the Mount Hood Iceberg dreams. Or the Big Pink Snail dreams. Or even the bathroom dreams. The images in my dreams are twisted and gory, bloody and deeply disturbing."

"Of all the difficulties working with dreams, trying to convince dreamers that the dreams they are able to recall are not personally theirs, and that these images are therefore not somehow reflections of the dreamer, is probably one of the most challenging. But remember what Thomas Mann has to say on the subject. In *The Magic Mountain* he writes:

> Now I know it is not out of our single souls we dream.
> We dream anonymously, communally, if each after his
> fashion. The great soul of which we are all a part may
> dream through us, in our manner of dreaming, its own
> secret dream . . .[9]

"Well, my fashion is gruesome then," says the dreamer.

"We could say it's your style," I add, smiling expansively.

"Great," the dreamer, along with everyone in the room, laughs.

"Ah, but wait," I say. "Remember that the word 'style' is related to the word 'stylus.' So style, in effect, is written across our foreheads at birth."

"So I'm *fated* to be gruesome?"

"Perhaps," I shrug. "But you're not being singled out, even though it might feel that way to you. And anyway, you're not *only* gruesome. In other words, gruesome, we could say, is one of your capacities for being. But you are never gruesome without being funny and sweet and generously spirited, smart and self-effacing and . . . the list goes on and on."

"Thank you," she says, sounding suddenly touched and genuinely relieved.

"It's important to remember that it's not what we do 'about' our fate, but rather what we do 'with' it that matters; it's this doing-within-fate that becomes the mark of us," I remind her. "Fate marks us, true enough, but what we do with how we are marked becomes the true mark of us."

Then, "Twenty-five years ago when I was studying to be an actor, Sandy Meisner turned to me and said, speaking through a hole in his throat where his larynx used to be, 'Did anyone ever tell you that you have a bizarre imagination?'"

The whole room bursts out laughing.

"Yeah, the entire acting class laughed then, too. But I was shocked, mortified, to discover that Sandy—who smoked still through that same hole in his throat—thought I had a 'bizarre imagination.' No one had ever said anything like that to me before. I left class that day twisted and wracked with what he might have meant, convinced that it had to mean that I must be a bizarre person. Not unique, not good at acting—bizarre and only bizarre. A few days later over drinks up at Sandy's house, I plucked up the courage to ask him. 'Sandy,' I said, 'you know how you said that I have a bizarre imagination?' 'Yes,' he said, through that same bizarre hole in his throat. 'Well, what do you mean by that exactly?' Then, before waiting for him to answer, as if I couldn't bear to hear what he might say, I stammered, 'Is that something I should . . . work on?' He shook his head in disgust then, like I had just asked the world's stupidest question, before turning to look me in the eye. Then, through a series of swallows and burps that were his only way of speaking, he pressed that little microphone on his throat and said, 'You couldn't change it if you tried. It's your gift. Your gold. But not until you figure out how to use it, how to give it. And, believe me, that's going to take some learning.'

"So, you see, it's the same with you. Having an instrument that lends itself to the macabre, or to the bizarre, or to the gruesome, only means that capacities of soul are trying to develop in you that make it possible for you to *bear* the macabre, the bizarre, the gruesome, the twisted, unnatural, and in pain. Gruesome then, for you, becomes a portal to the otherworld, to the world behind the world. But so long as you are trying to 'get away' from gruesome, gruesome will have no choice but to up the ante. Soul will have out. So a kind of psychological faith is necessary; one that trusts that Psyche is not out to get you, or any of us. And this, of course, requires that we surrender."

"It doesn't feel that way," says the dreamer.

"Of course not. That's why it's so important to educate the feelings. It's not enough to feel with the heart, we want to develop what the Sufis call a 'thinking heart.' But in order to do this, we have to educate those feelings that we commonly refer to as 'ours.'

"Remember the word 'educate' comes from the Latin, *educare*," I continue, "and it means, 'to lead out, to bring up, to rear.' So we want to rear the feeling life as we do our children, who, even though we give birth to them, are never really ours, right? From the time they are born, and even in utero, they are always utterly their own persons.

A Mother's Eye

This morning, as I was dropping my kids off at school,
I noticed, one by one, how dirty they were
in different ways:

My youngest had remnants of his breakfast
mixed with snot smeared across his cheek.
He was in the same clothes
he had picked out for himself yesterday,
still so proud that he insisted on sleeping in them
and doing it all over again.

Recognizing an opportunity for less laundry,
I didn't argue.

The next one, another boy, had foot-long fingernails
that were jagged and filthy and disgusting.
I cringed just looking at the beastly things.
But just as I was thinking that I should haul him
back into the car to cut them,
he flashed me the most dazzling smile
and I forgot my horror,
I forgot everything for a moment,
lost in the eternity of his dimple.

My girls, though slightly older,
weren't much better than the boys.
Clothes thrown together like a circus poster,
hair sticking up all over the place.
When I asked them what we should do about it,
my second one said, very matter-of-factly,
"I can't help that I have ecstatic hair, Mom."

What could I say to that?
My seven-year-old dervish
has hair that reaches up to God.

So I just stood there smiling
as I watched them walk away from me,
those four creatures that are mine
and yet somehow not mine at all,
the way they are so completely themselves,
utterly unconcerned
with the world of appearances.

And I was overcome then with a love so deep
and so real that my heart was near bursting.
And I thought, My God, they're beautiful.
How did I ever get so lucky?

When they say, "Mom, Mom, Mom,
watch me, watch me, watch this!"
I have never been fooled.

Children don't want to be watched—
they need to be seen.

What was it that Irish Philosopher once said?
To be, is to be perceived.
That's it, isn't it?

That's the secret that could very well
open the doors
of this unbearable culture of fear we've created.
The secret that could unlock
this prison of the manifest world
we've locked ourselves in.

If only we could turn a mother's eye
out toward all the children
of the world.

"It is likewise with feelings," I continue, "they are always their own beings. And they are only ever entrusted to our care. The task, therefore, is to handle them. But this doesn't mean to get a handle *on* them. It means developing the capacity to have 'gruesome,' for example, in our all-too-human hands, bearing it with our more-than-merely-human hearts—to lead out, to bring up, to rear Gruesome.

"So we ask: 'What does Gruesome want? What are its properties? Its features and characteristics? How does it sound in my chest, my throat, my mouth? How does it move through this body that now Gruesome and I share? What does Gruesome want, not only with me, and from me, but what does Gruesome want to do and say and show to me, and perhaps even through me? How may I serve this divine influx of Gruesome so that it is served by my words, my voice, and my movements? Have I the heart, the courage, to bear Gruesome in such a way that Gruesome is somehow redeemed by my willingness to serve it?"

"Then it's not so much that 'I' am gruesome but that I'm being asked to *attend* Gruesome?"

"Attend Gruesome, yes, with your heart—which is where we get the word 'courage,' from the Latin *coeur*, which, of course, means 'heart'— and it originally meant to tell the story of who you are with your whole heart. So have the heart to not turn away from your depths. Have the heart not to turn away from Gruesome. And what you'll begin to notice is that you can be deeply within the heart as an organ of perception and be present to the gruesome image in the dream without being taken hostage by it.

"Slowly a new kind of perceiving develops, that is, perceiving by means of heart-presence. The dream then will not be something that you've had; it will continue to happen, it will continue to unfold, to dream itself forward through you, and through this new kind of heart-perceiving."

Then, "There's a marvelous story that comes to us from Henry Corbin regarding Ibn Arabi, the great Sufi mystic and philosopher, and his reaction to the story of Joseph's dream. It goes like this."

TA'WIL AND JOSEPH DREAMING

Once upon a time, when Joseph was still a child, he said to his father, "Eleven stars and the sun and the moon were prostrating themselves before me in a dream last night."

Many years later, and near the end of the story, when Joseph is a man and acting as the vizier in charge of all the land in Egypt, he welcomes his brothers to the Pharaoh's land. Not recognizing Joseph as their brother, the brothers prostrate themselves before him, whereupon Joseph declares, "This is the interpretation of my old vision. The Lord has fulfilled it."

The word used in the Koran for "interpretation" is *ta'wil*.

But now, the problem with Joseph's statement for Ibn Arabi, according to Henry Corbin, is simply that it's not true. For Joseph imagines that he's found the hidden meaning of his dream in the events that happened with his brothers prostrating themselves like the moon and stars of his boyhood dream. But *ta'wil* does not consist of bringing the realm of the imaginal down to the human level of concrete things in order to "make sense" of the images. For this would be to destroy the truth of the imagination. Instead, the task is "to proceed in the opposite direction." In other words, we are charged with the task of carrying the sensible forms back to the imaginative forms whence they came.

For Ibn Arabi, therefore, the *ta'wil* that Joseph thought he'd discovered was not *ta'wil* at all, for it was nothing more than the work of a man who was still sleeping. In other words, though Joseph dreamt that he had awakened from a dream, through his interpretation we discover that Joseph had, in fact, not awakened at all. For humans, according to the Koran, are asleep. And it is only at our deaths that we awaken.

"Don't we all do that Joseph thing?" I ask then. "Don't we all try to make waking-world sense of things?" Then, turning to the woman attending Gruesome, "So, you see, to dream of something gruesome is not a suggestion of one's gruesomeness. And, according to the story we've just heard, it would be a mistake to proceed in this direction as though it were. Instead, we are asked to get very curious about the light behind Gruesome and what it wants."

"Just hearing that this dream is not a reflection of how gruesome I am is a tremendous relief," says the dreamer.

"I'm confused," another in the group suddenly interjects. "How do we educate our feelings?"

"Psychotherapy, as it is all-too-commonly practiced, asks, in that terribly 'significant' tone, which always seems to accompany that terribly 'significant' face: *'How does that make you feel?'* And from there we are invited to talk about how we feel with the therapist. Nothing drives me madder! For this is almost always an invitation to abstraction, actually away from the feeling life in a living body—which is not the body as a specimen or the body as a physical object in space—but a body that sighs and loves, one that shudders and cries, that aches and longs to be touched in a certain way, or not—a *living* body. And it's through this living body that we are in touch with the feeling life. So any invitation to talk 'about' feelings moves us away from the feeling life into abstraction. But it's the feeling of the feeling life in a living body that is so directional, so guiding, so wisdom filled.

"Oh, and wouldn't you know it. Dear old Susan Wright has just walked in the room," I laugh and shake my head. "All right, Ms. Wright, perhaps another wee story . . ."

"Don't Call Yourself an Actress Unless . . ."

Susan was a member the very talented and highly regarded Wright family, an entire family of actors that included Janet, Anne, and John, though it was Susan who was the crown jewel of the Canadian stage. She played all the major stages, including many seasons at Stratford. And oh, she was a fine, magnificent actor. Her powerful and moving portrayal of the tragic protagonist in Brecht's *Mother Courage* remains indelibly branded on the hearts of all who had the great good fortune to be in her audience.

Susan was one of those rarest of creatures with an incredible natural command of a room. Ever the actress, she loved an audience, but she also had the kind of talent and largess, presence and charisma to know what to do with an audience, for their sake as well as hers. And she had a damn good, that is, *naturally* good, voice.

The word "awe" means equal parts beauty and terror; I can think of no better word to describe the experience of being in Susan's presence. She was a powerful force to be reckoned with and I was in complete and utter jaw-dropping awe of her.

Once, when I was about twenty years old, I was invited to a very small dinner party for her, with only about eight or so guests. But numbers didn't matter—eight or eighty—if Susan was in the room, she always held court.

Some time into the evening, well into her cups, after many a ribald story, and with her personal life turned into explicitly displayed dramas in which she was at once all the players, the director, the producer, the costume designer, the props manager, the lighting guy, the ticket taker, the usher, *and* the audience, Susan suddenly turned her attention to me and said, "So you want to be an actress, eh?"

I thought I'd die. Through her touching, tactile gaze, it was as if I was being felt up, all over and very intimately, only on the inside. No one had ever looked at me quite like that before.

"Well, let me tell you something about being an actress," she said, suddenly springing to her feet while lifting her drink hand dramatically into the air. Then, "I THINK WITH MY CUNT!" she bellowed, pounding on her pudendum with the wadded, tight fist of her cigarette hand to make the exclamation point. Then, with her drink hand still dramatically poised in the air, she pointed at me with her smoking hand, narrowed her eyes, and said, "DON'T call yourself an ACTRESS unless you can THINK with your *CUNT!*" And again she pounded the exclamation point on her pudendum. "Got it?" she said.

Oh, let me tell you, I got it. In fact, I don't think I ever got a better acting lesson in all the years of studying to be an actor than this. Susan was her words. They came out of her every orifice, out of her knees, her elbows, her neck, the folds of her skin, even her eyelashes and hair. In the absence of spoken words, you could read her like a book. Emotion poured through her like music from the double-reeded aulos of Dionysus himself. Hot, now cold, then gold, now honey-sweet, strong and intoxicating, she was like a river, burning. And there wasn't an ounce of her that wasn't wisdom-earth, as if she was the last of the oak-seers, the Druids, or as if the clay of her had been molded from the foundational earth surrounding the Delphic Oracle. When she turned her gaze toward you, it was as though she was cross-pinning you to a mounting board before adding you to her specimen collection. And if you were careful, or wise, or, as in my case, just plain lucky, you listened and got the gift she was trying to give you. But it was the strength of her educated feeling life that always guided her.

⁓

"Okay, but she was a natural at it, right?" one of the dreamers asks. "I mean, how does one begin to think with their . . ." she glances somewhat uncomfortably around the room.

"Cunt?" I offer then.

She laughs and turns crimson.

"Well, not literally, for one thing. In other words, this isn't something that's only open to women. Oh," I say then, unable to help myself, "no pun intended."

When the room settles down, I continue, "But if even the word is difficult to say—because we think it's wrong or bad or offensive or whatever—chances are we're not thinking with it. Chances are that the usual puritanical overlay, so prevalent in America, is getting in the way. We have terribly Puritan ideas of what it means to live a purified life. But remember the word purification originally meant 'excluding nothing.' Well, Susan was the queen of excluding nothing.

"Now it's true, she wasn't terribly intent on practicing soul purification, but she was an unequaled master of the feeling life—an oracular poet of the living body. And she was trying to teach me, in just those few sentences and gestures, how to become a life-long student of the educated feeling life. It was her gift to me and I'm still thanking her.

"The difference that's being alluded to has everything to do with moving out of a closed system—one that practices life as a kind of enactment, out of what we think things should be, or ought to be—and into ever-opening receptivity. This is why 'cunt,' as Susan so rightly, so earthily intuits, is such a good image. Because it's the *vesica piscis*, the portal to the otherworld, through these living bodies. Now, as it turns out, the otherworld is precisely the same as this world only filled with the essence of being that cannot be seen on this side except through fantasy, that is, until we begin to make our way through that imaginal portal."

"Wait a minute, can we go back," someone in the group says. "I'm still stuck on why we want to rear Gruesome?"

"Because it's part of what it means to be human."

"But does it have to be?" she asks. "I mean . . . we're not *trying* to be gruesome or anything, are we?"

"No, of course not. But it is part of what it means to be human. Where we usually get into trouble is by trying to exclude something that we don't like or that we don't want to include in what is already included in what it means to be human."

The look on her face indicates that this is a very distasteful notion, one that goes against all that she's been taught. "Let's see if we can open this up," I suggest.

THE DAY THE MOTHERS STOOD UP

Everyone talks about how hard it is to be a mother, but they make it seem as though it's all the laundry that needs folding, the colic that needs soothing, the nipples cracked and re-cracking, bleeding each time the baby latches on, and the seemingly endless nights without sleep. And these are difficult enough, especially after a difficult labor and delivery, when hormones stampede though our broken-and-stitched, newly initiated bodies. Yet even the most overwhelming aspects of these pale in comparison with the crushing realization that our children have entirely separate fates over which we have no control.

I knew I would love her. I already did. But when the doctor plunked her on my belly, still covered in the blood of being born, beautiful and wide-eyed and already curious about the startling world she'd chosen to enter, I was overcome with a devastating love for her that was only equaled by an overwhelming sense of vulnerability. In birthing her, I had likewise given birth to her eventual death. And it was this realization, sudden and crushing, that birthed me as a mother. It was almost more than I could bear.

But before long, something even more unexpected began to happen. She was perhaps three months old when it started. Knives were a particular horror. I'd pass by the kitchen and notice the gray glint of a paring knife resting on the countertop and I'd be overcome suddenly with a desire to pick it up and plunge it into her tiny chest. Or I'd be hanging some new picture up in her room and I'd glance over at the hammer on her dresser and wonder then, almost casually, what it might be like to smash her tiny skull with it. Or I'd be out walking around the neighborhood proudly showing her off in her bright and shiny, red-tartan stroller, all bundled up and exquisitely beautiful, when we'd come to the top of a very steep hill, and all I could think of then was what it would it be like to let go and let her stroller career out of control, down the hill.

Yet I never once considered my daughter in any "real" physical danger. I never once imagined I might actually stab her or plunge my fingers into her eye sockets. I was never—and I mean not even once—afraid for what I might actually do. I never imagined that I might be one of those women pasted across the front of grocery line tabloids—*Post-Partum Mom Knifes Newborn*—but I was nevertheless utterly terrified of the images that were presenting, and perhaps even more terrified of telling anyone about them for fear that my daughter might be taken away from me.

At the same time, I became concerned that by not allowing the phenomenon of the images to unfold, that I might be inadvertently inflicting some sort of unconscious psychic damage on my daughter. I felt impelled to try to grapple with the images, at least on the most rudimentary level. Perhaps initially motivated by a desire to conquer them, I found myself more and more curious about the images themselves, the way one gets curious about certain dream images. Curiosity, as it turns out, is a stronger motivator than fear.

Having never suffered from a phobia, I thought it best to start secretly by examining phobias in general. I learned that phobias are the emotional and physical reactions to feared objects or situations. I read that symptoms include:

- Feelings of panic, horror, dread, or terror. *Check.*
- A recognition that the fear goes beyond the normal boundaries of the actual threat of danger. *Check.*
- Reactions that are automatic and uncontrollable, practically taking over the person's thoughts. *Check.*
- A rapid heartbeat, shortness of breath, trembling, and an overwhelming desire to flee the situation—all the physical reactions of extreme fear are commonly present. *Check.*

    — Extreme measures are frequently taken to avoid the
    feared object or situation. *Check.*

    Though I could check all of these so-called symptoms either alone or
grouped together, I never once considered myself sick. Naturally, I feared
that by not considering myself sick I was almost certainly sick, but, at the
same time, it struck me that the phenomenon of the images and the way
that they were presenting themselves was not something that I needed
to "recover" from. Rather, they seemed aimed at something, pointing
toward something purposive. In other words, I had the strong sense that
besides just trying to get my full and immediate attention, the images
were also trying to show me something, something that would take all of
my patience and courage not to turn away from, and, if not for me, then
for the sake of my infant daughter.

    As I began to get more and more interested in the images, to look
at them more closely and to regard them, simply, and without judgment,
a curious thing happened. I started noticing when the images appeared
and how long they lingered. Little by little, image by image, I began to
develop a certain respect for them, and before long I became a kind of
keeper of them.

    Soon I was able to examine the "image" I was striving to present
to the world and I began to wonder if the infanticidal images weren't
soul's way of crushing my fantasies of being a perfect mother? And so it
was that in my struggle to be a less-than-perfect mother, a good-enough
mother, I allowed the images to knife and hammer their way into my
day, and to careen down the hill of my heroic consciousness. Instead of
turning away from them, I carried them around as I might the images in a
dream (if I'd been sleeping enough at night to remember any dreams).

    After several weeks of this, and feeling less as though the images
"had" me, I decided to call my sister to ask if she'd experienced anything
similar when she became a mother.

"I couldn't get through the first line of *You are My Sunshine* without bawling my head off," she laughed. "But no," she said then, "I never fantasizing about crushing his skull. His father's maybe, but not his."

"Don't get me started," I chimed in, laughing.

Then, "I'm not afraid of the height of heights," my sister explained, as our talk turned to phobias. "I'm afraid of the overwhelming urge to jump. A different sort of swoon seizes me. I feel drawn over the edge, as if the void were calling me. It's not a death wish," she said, sounding convinced and as though this was not the first time she'd thought about the subject. "I am petrified by the impulse; it's like this seductive urge to let go and fly and it won't be blinked away. It's why I don't trust myself in high places."

"Is it only the falling that you imagine?"

"Or the jumping," she added.

"But never the crash?"

"Never. I never imagine myself dead. In other words, the crash doesn't call to me like the invitation to 'float' does. Rationally, of course, I know that a crash at the bottom would follow my inability to resist the invitation to float, so I shy away from high places. I simply can't trust myself not to be 'invited' over the edge."

"I feel a similar invitation," I said, imagining myself standing on a very high balcony looking down, or from way up the Eiffel Tower. "I find it weirdly exhilarating, though, the tension between wanting to fall and my resistance to it. But perhaps I don't feel it as strongly as you do? I never imagine that I might actually jump."

"Or I imagine that there will be a catastrophic earthquake at the exact moment I peer over the edge of a cliff and 'ahhhhhhhhhhhhh,' down I go," she snorted. "I can't ride in the passenger seat on a trip through the mountains for the same reason. I have to be behind the wheel, at night, with my eyes riveted to the road in front of me."

"So is it a fear of death?"

"Death is in it, perhaps, or behind it, lingering, but I don't have to die, or almost die, to know that I don't want to. I think I have all the normal fears of death, of dying before I am ready, of dying painfully, of leaving my children motherless. But it's not my death that calls to me from great heights; it's the free-float before that I find so all-inviting."

"Like the free-float of amniotic fluid before being born into the crushing world of time and space."

"Ha!" she laughed. "I remember neither the dull nor the gory details of being a kid, and you want me to recall the physical sensations surrounding me in the womb?"

"I'm just trying to come at it mythologically," I explained after we'd both had a good laugh. "So the crash at the bottom is absent from the experience of the call coming to you from the void . . ."

"Um-hum."

"The same way that my baby's lifeless little body is not present in the images that steel and steal their way into my conscious world."

"If you say so," she sounded unconvinced of any connection.

A few months later, I was at school with my daughter, whom I was still nursing. In a History of Depth Psychology class we were discussing Freud, the myth of Oedipus, and the Oedipal complex, when one of my classmates, a man, and himself the father of two grown children, piped up. "I just don't buy it," he said. "The whole myth is so far-fetched. I mean, what mother would agree to killing her infant child?" He motioned toward me. "I saw you nursing your baby on the break, Renée," he said, "We all saw it. And we could see the love between the two of you—it was dripping off of you."

"That was my milk," I quipped.

"That connection, the deep, deep connection between a mother and her child is evident in the way you are with one another," he shook his head. "And I'm sorry. I just don't think a mother would do what this mother, this *Jocasta*," he practically spat her name out, "does in the myth—give her son to a herdsman to kill because she's afraid that he might grown up to kill his father. No way. Freud was wrong to pick this myth as *the* myth. No mother in her right mind would do that. What sort of mother would consider killing her baby?" He gestured toward me dramatically while waiting for a response from the rest of the students.

Well, hell, I'm all but sure I would not have offered up a confession on my own, but what could I say to such an open invitation? It was so innocent and well intentioned on his part. Perhaps if he'd used someone else as his exemplar I could have just sat there casually nodding my head, pretending to agree. But with me as his case-in-point model mother, I reluctantly decided that it was in the best interest of those gathered to tell the truth about the infanticidal images that had been presenting themselves to me.

"Actually," I said, taking a defeated breath, as I began the piteously slow task of unpacking the death-dark contents I'd been secretly spiriting around for the last three months.

An excruciating pall came over the room, as the class—which was made up of about twenty-two graduate students, six men and the rest women, all older than me by a generation or more—sat utterly transfixed, listening to my twisted confessional. No one said a word. Then the most extraordinary thing happened: one by one every mother in that room slowly and quite deliberately stood up, until they were all standing.

"I am seventy-four years old," said Jeanne, the silver-haired matriarch of the group, in a thick French accent. "And I've kept what happened to me a secret for fifty years." She looked me boldly in the eye. "Fifty years! I used to lock myself in the bathroom and count to ten, praying that I wouldn't do what I imagined doing to my children, it was so horrible. *And I was horrible*, I thought, a terrible mother for thinking such things! I knew there was no worse sin in the world so I kept it hidden and tried to forget about it. I told no one. Not my mother. Not my husband. Not even the priest. No one. Until today."

"I forgot. Somehow I *managed* to forget," Mara, the middle-aged mother standing next to Jeanne, started slowly. "It gets easier you know, when the kids get older. You get so busy running them to birthday parties and Boy Scouts and soccer games. I made sure I kept myself busy. Then I divorced and divorced again. And oh, I got frustrated and lost my temper, even raged because it was so difficult at times," she shook her head, "but nothing was like what I experienced in those first few months. That was . . ." she trailed off, unable to find words to convey the unspeakable. Then, suddenly brightening, "I'm pleased to report that my kids are all beautifully grown up, healthy and as well-adjusted, or not, you know," she chuckled, "as the next person. But it was so damn brutal, so demoralizing at the beginning. So much more than I could handle, and yet somehow I did."

"When I think about it," said Christine, "it's almost like a miracle that my kids are here. What kept me from acting on those impulses? Was it luck? Fear? Grace?" She struggled to hold back her tears. "I've never told a single soul what I went through. I was convinced that something was wrong with me, I mean, really wrong, *crazy* wrong, you know? Mixed up. And that if I wasn't careful, ever-vigilant, I'd do something criminal and end up like those women you read about. I was shocked by my . . ." she hesitated. "I felt so inept, unable to cope, and I was terrified I'd end up like *that*. But I never told anyone. I never let on that I was overwhelmed. Even when my daughter had her own daughter and was clearly overwhelmed by the experience, I kept my mouth shut," she shook her head then turned to look at me. *"Why? Why did I do that?"*

And on it went for the rest of the afternoon, with every one of those mothers making her tortured confession. And we stood there witnessing one another in great sorrow and even greater pity, listening and crying rivers of cleansing tears. And there was even room for laughter then, and finally, after all the stories had been told, we were restored again to ourselves—not without our darkness, but perhaps *because* of it, and because of our willingness to suffer alone and then how we risked suffering together, each of us held by the other and for the other, and by the threads of the dark delicate tapestry we dared to weave into that room.

As for the women not mothers and the men gathered there that day, well, they held up the sacred corners, knowing that they were part of something entirely rare—witnessing and weaving the darkest of the dark, and yet exquisite, terrible and tortured, and undeniably beautiful—as if the veil between the two worlds had been lifted and we were all given a chance to make something of the way things really are for an afternoon.

≈

"Is this what you mean by educating the feeling life?" one of the dreamers asks in disbelief.

"Partially," I answer. "But it's all too psychological when we hear it like this."

Nothing Apart From Her

If it is written across your forehead
that you will meet your end
in fire,
you needn't be afraid
of water,
said the old soothsayer,
looking into my cup.

What at times is more inviting
than the weightlessness of hair

floating up
underwater
out toward the promise
of the Great Mother?
But weighted to birth,
through this body in time,
there's no possibility
of a back-crawl towards
Oblivion,
only the crush
of what it means
to be Mothered
by She Who Holds
the Sword and Noose.
And all the firewater in the world
won't stop that crush
no matter how long
you drink it.

The desire to jump
from very high places
is first felt by those
with the urge to climb,
and it won't be blinked away;
for The Red-Eyed One—
She who holds
the severed head
in Her hand—
brings us into being
and calls us
to our deaths.

An exquisitely beautiful woman
heavy with child
steps from the river
to give birth.
Tenderly

she nurses the newborn
at her breast.
A moment later,
she seizes the child
in her jaws
and crushes it,
before disappearing
back into the water.

All-creating,
All-nourishing,
All-devouring.

Don't call yourself a devotee
if, in the presence
of my ritual nakedness,
you do not feel
the same terrifying emotion
that I first felt before this revelation.
Then there is no rite at all,
only a secular act—
wide-mouthed fucking—
with all the familiar
consequences.

"The trick is to feel our way into it," I continue. "But first we have to feel our way into what's actually there, what's actually present. For it seems that a good deal of the time we're either pretending that what's actually there isn't, or we're busy trying to ignore it because it's not what we've come to think should be present, or it's not how it's supposed to be, or we're busy trying to manifest something we think ought to be present instead, or, or, or . . . there are any number of reasons we turn away from feeling, that is, from experiencing, what's actually there."

Then, "When we hear the word 'feeling' it's easy to assume that we're talking about 'feelings,' which is another word we commonly use for the emotions. Emotions are included in this kind of feeling, but it's rather more akin to feeling our way along in the dark."

How I Learned to Love the Dark

When I was a kid we had a basement and, like so many basements in Saskatchewan at the time, it was just a plain, ugly, oversized cinderblock, with nothing but a furnace in one corner, and, on a wall perpendicular to that, a deep-freeze which sat next to a washing machine and spin dryer.

Now to jazz it up, my father managed to get a hold of a bunch of paint-sale paint. And he proceeded then to paint the entire floor in an electric, tangerine orange color, on top of which he painted several games in a bright, vibrant blue. The effect was really quite spectacular, very well done, and a lot of fun. There was a hopscotch game, I remember, and Twister, and Hoppie-Toppie, which was rather like hopscotch only played with a hockey puck.

We were shuffled down there to play during those cold winter months when the forty-below temperatures outside forced us indoors. I suspect it was my parents' way to keep us kids away from the adult life in the house. All of our toys were down there so it was just this vast, brightly colored space within which we could hang out and play.

Now, I am the younger of two girls; my sister is eighteen months older, and we have a brother who is five years younger than me, so at this point he was sort of too young to play with. Anyway, I was always dying to get my older sister to play with me. And, being my sister, she would use this against me.

"Gernoz!" she'd holler. "Gernoz!"

She called me "Gernoz"—some made-up name she gave me because I picked my nose and "Gernoz," according to my sister, had some similarity of sound with the word "nostril."

"Gernoz!" she'd say. "Come play Hoppie-Toppie!"

Well, as soon as I'd hear this, I'd zip downstairs as fast as my little legs could zip, so excited that she was finally willing to play with me. And then we'd start playing. We'd get a few minutes into the game— which I was always losing because she made up the rules as she went along and they were always to her advantage—when my sister would say, "Oh, I gotta go pee." And without hesitating then, she'd dash up the stairs as if she were going to go to the bathroom. But instead of going anywhere, she'd stay at the top of the stairs, turn the lights off, and say, "Ooooooooooohhhhhhhhhhhh," making scary ghost noises that were guaranteed to terrify me.

Now, it was Halloween-cat black down there in the dark of that basement. There were only two teeny tiny windows—which were only big enough to slither through should there ever be a house fire—that were located at the top of the wall on the washer and dryer side. But by this time of the year they were completely covered over in snow, so there was absolutely no light whatsoever coming in from anywhere. It was so dark that it was actually disorienting.

I'd scream then as I made my terrified way over to the stairs before bounding up two or three at a time. When I neared the top, my sister would casually turn the light on and act as though she was just returning from the bathroom. "Gernoz," she'd ask, all innocent-like, "what's the matter?"

If she were really lucky, I'd make such a fuss about the whole thing that my parents would eventually come over and give me royal hell for being too dramatic and ridiculously over-emotional. And all the while my sister would stand there—the picture of innocence and sanity, and of calm, rational behavior—while I wailed on about the "Oooooohhhhh" of ghosts and trolls.

I can't tell you how many times this was repeated for my sister's rather sadistic pleasure. But one day, perhaps when my father was yelling at me to pull myself together, I finally decided that I'd had enough, and that if my sister ever attempted anything like that again, I simply would not give her the satisfaction of seeing me suffer.

So one day, "Gernoz!" she hollered. "Gernoz! Come play Hoppie-Toppie!" And I raced to play with her just as I always had.

Only this time when we got to the twos in the game and she said, "Oh, I gotta go pee," I was prepared. When she turned the lights out and began her ghostly wail, "Oooooooooooohhhhhhhhhhh," I was just as terrified as ever, but equally resolved not to give my sister the same old satisfaction. Slowly then, I made my way over to the closest wall. It was no more than a few steps away, but it took several lifetimes to get there— with every imaginable demon and ghost, monster and troll assailing me through the deep, dark disorientation of that place.

When I finally reached the wall and felt that concrete, though cold as a winter grave, it was terribly soothing and reassuring, familiar and yet utterly unfamiliar at the same time. I knew it was the wall of our basement, but I had never experienced it quite like that before. I immediately became interested in feeling the wall's every bump and crag, nook and cranny, like a blind person might feel another's face in order to know something about that person.

With each new feeling handful, as I inched my way around the circumference of the basement, I gathered more . . . what? Information? Yes. But it was more than that, and more than knowledge, too. It was a kind of *feeling* wisdom, as though, through my willingness to go at things this way, the Darkness was revealing some of her best-kept secrets to me. And it was incredibly powerful.

As I fingered my feeling way along, I lost all sense of even being in the dark. Which is not to say that I lost a sense of the dark; I did not. But what I did lose, for the most part, was the sense of being separate from it. In other words, I became part of the dark. Or perhaps Dark Renée was revealed to me. And I was offered images then, all sorts of images, as a kind of dark feasting, as if I were eating my way through the underworld, through what had been, only moments before, monsters and demons, goblins and trolls, and my almost paralyzing fear.

It was as though I'd fallen through fear to what's on the other side of it. But what's on the other side of it is exactly the same as what's on this side, only lit from within, and without the emotional grip. So all of the same things were there, only I no longer experienced them as terrifying. What an extraordinary thing!

By the time I got to the stairs that led to the floor above, I lifted my head and ascended those steps slowly, one by one. Half-way up the stairs, as per usual, my sister flicked the light on and pretended then to be arriving back from the bathroom. This time, however, things were different. I stopped at the top of the stairs just long enough to look my sister straight in the eye, triumphantly, before proceeding past her. She never ever asked me to play Hoppie-Toppie again.

"So when we talk about the feeling life, it is this sort of thing to which I'm referring. It's not that there isn't emotion in it. There is. But it's much more akin to feeling our way along in the dark, in living bodies. And this is where the heart comes in. For the heart is an invaluable guiding instrument in this dark, feeling region. It's utterly navigational."

"Do you remember any of the images that presented themselves to you when you were down there?"

"Everything had a luminous, moonlit quality and I remember thinking that it was strange that things would be lit by the moon down there in our basement like that. But then again, the moon had always been my friend, my companion—as it is for so many children—so it no longer seemed so strange that it would turn up when its companionship was what I needed most."

"I'm curious about what you said about the heart being a guiding instrument," the woman attending Gruesome says. "In what way?"

"Through love," I answer. "It was love that made me decide to finally stand up to my sister's torment. And it was my heart as an organ of perception that fed me those luminous images the entire time I was down there in that basement. It was the heart that fed and comforted and encouraged me along. It was likewise the gushing love I experienced when my daughter was born that presented all those knives and the horror around hammers. But it was a greater love still that kept me looking at those same images long enough to be able to see through them to what was, to what is, on the other side. Though perhaps I should mention that it didn't feel like love going through it.

"So this is precisely where the details of the dream, of Gruesome, for example, do indeed play a part," I continue. "For 'gruesome' as merely an adjective is far too abstract. Instead, you are being asked to become Gruesome's attendant through repulsive or grisly images that evoke your horror specifically, an altogether unique-to-you specificity. But it's at this very juncture that we have to be most careful, most delicate, where we need to proceed with extreme caution. For the specificity of the image— the exactness of Gruesome—can become distracting at precisely this point. We don't want the knives or the hammers or whatever the images are to become reduced to merely kitchen knives and household hammers or to things from the concrete world of things only. This would be to experience the dream image as 'idol.' As 'icon,' on the other hand, we begin to see *through* the images specifically to what capacities of soul we are being asked to uniquely develop."

ANCESTORS DREAMING

Once upon a time, Karen sat across from me with a book in her lap. She said, "I know you don't have much time for novels, but I'd really like you to read this one."

"Oh?"

"It's about a woman who makes death masks of people who are either about to die or of people who have recently died. And it made me think of you."

"Death masks?"

"Yeah, like the ones you make from dreams only these are left behind for the living, to help the living stay connected to their dead," Karen said, handing me the book. As I received the book into my hands, it was as if the whole room rippled. And I knew right away that this exchange had something to do with my destiny.

What we didn't know then, Karen and I, was that within a month of this exchange, Karen's mother would die.

On Boxing Day, Karen and her family were scheduled to come over to our house to hang out for the holidays. Sometime during the day, as I was making preparations to receive them, I got a call from Karen telling me that her mother—who had recently undergone hip surgery to repair her broken hip—had been re-hospitalized and that it didn't look good. By the next day, her mother was gone.

Oh, but there's another part to this. At a recent luncheon for a local ladies group that I belong to, my business card was selected from a fish bowl of business cards to receive a free "energy healing" session. I had no idea what an energy healing entailed, but I thought I'd at least try to have some sort of experience of it to see if there was any way that I could support this woman in the practice of her work. So off I went, reluctantly, I'll admit, for my free energy healing in the days leading up to Christmas.

Well, I'm not entirely sure what happened during that session—I mean, I have no idea really of what she did, and perhaps even less of an idea of what I actually experienced, but it definitely involved stillness and rest. She did some Reiki and some "painting over me" with some special "energy" crystals.

I left there exhausted, feeling torpid and indolent and heavy and yet, somehow, strangely returned to myself. I've participated in enough ritual over the years to know that these things have rippling effects, so I just got curiouser and curiouser.

The heaviness continued. All I could manage for the most part over the holidays was playing table games with my kids, cooking a bit, reading, and a lot of sleeping. And yet this seemed to be all that was being asked of me. A few days into this, I had the distinct feeling that this was a preparation for something, but I had no clue what.

And then Karen's mother died.

The following afternoon I took my kids out to a local large cat rescue center for a tour that we had booked several months before. Shambala is a lion and tiger, leopard and liger, large cat sanctuary run by the actress Tippi Hedren of *The Birds* fame. The tour was just for the kids, so whilst the kids were inside with the big cats, parents were asked to wait outside.

The rain let up and the weather was glorious, so I sat in the car with the windows rolled down, breathing in the rain-soaked fresh air while reading Peter Kingsley's *Reality*. I was taken with the part where the author talks about Parmenides' poem—about longing and desire and dream incubation— and I was particularly struck then with the playing of pipes in the poem. He was discussing the hissing of the snake and the noises necessary to enter a dream-like trance state—and I was contemplating this in terms of dream practices.

At a certain point, I became very aware that out there in the middle of nowhere, two very distinct hissing noises could be heard. I listened carefully and discovered that one of the hissing noises was being made by the wind rustling through the dried leaves on all the trees, and the other came from a rushing stream that had been created by all the recent rains.

I got out of the car then and walked down to the stream. I stood there for what seemed a good long while and I thought about stillness and dream incubation. And I thought too about Karen's mother. And as I stood there allowing the sound of that stream to penetrate, from behind me there came quite a palaver.

I turned and saw *The Birds* literally circling around the top of a strange-looking hill—there must have been thirty or so ravens and they were making one heck of a caw, caw, cawing racket and quite a display with their antics—flying in circles, fighting, teasing one another, and cavorting. And I wondered then what it must be like for Tippi Hedren to experience this? And as I was imagining this, a raven left this bunch of circling black birds and flew directly over my head, close enough for me to hear the whoosh of the flapping wings and feel the fanning of flown-through air move around me. I had to laugh; Raven is one of my totems. Though I always pay particular attention to what's occurring during these kinds of visitations, I'll admit I didn't think too terribly much of it, at least not the first time it happened.

But then it happened again, in almost exactly the same way, and then again. No other birds flew off in any other direction. No other birds flew over anyone else walking around the place. Only me. By the third time, the oracular nature of Raven's visit was undeniable, but I couldn't imagine what it was about.

Later that afternoon, as I was cutting up some butternut squash to make soup for Karen's grieving family, it suddenly hit me. I put down the knife and called her immediately. "Karen," I said, "what do you think about making a death mask of your mother?"

There was a short pause. "Okay," she said.

"I mean, do you think it's possible even?"

"I don't know."

"Well, I could do it alone, or you could accompany me, that is, if you want to. It's up to you."

"I'd like to do it with you," she said without hesitation. "I'll call the guy at the crematorium to see if it's possible."

Now the guy at the crematorium is another story. His name is Steven. When the hospital handed Karen a six-page-long list of places to choose from, she picked a local place that specializes in cremations, having no idea at all one from the other.

When she and her sister went to meet the director of the place, however, they were immediately struck with a vague sense of recognition. Turns out that twenty years earlier, when Karen and her sister were making arrangements for their father's burial at sea through the Neptune Society up in San Francisco, this very same fellow was the guy who handled all of the arrangements for them. *Coincidence?* Heeding the call to offer bare minimum services to those who want or need them, Steven left the Neptune Society because he felt that even they were charging too much for death-related services.

So Karen called Steven and asked for permission to make a death mask of her mother. Though he admitted that he'd never before had a similar request, he said that he was open to the idea and that he would check on the condition of her mother's body. The following morning I got a call from Karen saying that we were good to go. "But," she added, "obviously, the sooner the better."

We were scheduled to work together that afternoon for our regular dream tending session so I suggested we do it then.

"Okay," she said. "What do we need to do?"

"Shower," I replied. It just sort of tumbled out. Then, "We need to cleanse ourselves in order to work with her body." I don't know why I said this; I'd never worked with a dead body before. In fact, I'd never even seen one, except at a distance under a white sheet, after a highway accident. I'd only ever been to one or two funerals, and I didn't know the deceased.

"Anything else?" asked Karen.

I can't think of anything right now. I have all the materials—I'll throw them together and see you at three."

"Okay," she said. "I'll pick you up."

Apart from throwing the things together that we would need, and the shower, I had very little time to consider what we were about to do; I had absolutely no idea what to expect. Neither did Karen, and we talked about this on the way over to the crematorium.

"Do you think it will be creepy?"

"It might be," I said. Then, "I imagine it's going to be different for us. She's your mother. Well, not really your mother, but your mother's body. If it gets too creepy for you or too emotional or . . . you can leave."

Just then the rain stopped and the sun started to peek out from behind a large cloud. "Oh look!" Karen suddenly said. "There's a rainbow." And there it was—the most glorious, over-arching double rainbow. We both felt very encouraged by seeing it.

Before long we were at the crematorium. Karen introduced me to Steven and without any delay he led us to a small adjoining room, and there, laid out in a coffin-shaped cardboard box, was the body of Karen's mother; I was immediately struck by her intense beauty. Then Steven asked us if we needed anything.

"Only water," I motioned toward the bathroom that was located behind him. "Everything else we have." We set up twelve votive candles then and Karen lit them for the spirit of her mother as she made her way over to the other side. Then we set up some mementos that Karen had brought with her and we got down to work.

I placed a scarf around her mother's delicate white hair to protect it from the plaster material, just like I do with the living. In fact, the way we were with her body was as though she were still living. Strangely, and beautifully, and quite unexpectedly, it was impossible for it to be any other way. As I smeared the Vaseline across the surface of her mother's fine-boned face, the experience was so deeply moving that I can hardly put words to it.

None of the creepiness was there. No spookiness, no heebie-jeebies, no skin crawling, and nothing whatsoever like it—only beauty of the rarest sort, accompanied by incredible tenderness, rather like I experienced when each of my children were born. And Karen felt it too. It's not a wonder that back when we still knew how to do death-related things, it was the midwives who also prepared the bodies for burial after death. What a sad loss it is for us that this tenderest of connections with death is all but gone.

The thing that struck me the most, however, was the holiness of the body itself. I had always imagined that it was the soul-spirit-life in a body that made it something holy, that the soul-spirit-life gave the body its interiority. And I assumed that when the soul-spirit-life was no longer present that the body would cease to be holy, that it would be rather like a husk or a disposable thing of sorts. I don't mean this in a crass way. I just never had the experience to think otherwise until I began making the death mask.

And then Steven came into the room and asked to watch what we were doing. He stood there quietly for a long while as we layered strips of plaster cast material across the entire surface of her delicate face. "I find this incredibly moving," he whispered. "Do you do this a lot?"

I explained that I had been making masks for over fifteen years but that this was the first mask that I'd ever made on a body that was no longer living. Then, as we waited for the mask to cure—which took quite a bit longer than it does on a living body due to the body's temperature lending itself to the curing process, I suppose—we talked about death, and the business of death, Steven's calling, and dreams.

Eventually the mask cured up beautifully and when we lifted it off it was an incredible thing to behold. As we cleaned the remaining plaster from her mother's face and hair, we were all of us again struck by the intense beauty of the experience. And I began to understand what the opening was about during the holiday season; all the tenderizing was preparation for this. Life is truly strange and beautiful and so unexpected. Oh, if only we could learn to open ourselves to it.

"So then," the dreamer hesitates, not sure how to word her question, "*this* is feeling? Is it the beauty of the experience or . . ."

"The whole thing," I answer. "Beauty is part of it, but so is the novel that I didn't read with the character in it who makes death masks, the rippling room, the 'energy healing' and the undoing of all my heroic doing, Tippi Hedren and *The Birds*, the book on dream incubation and stillness, Karen's mother, Karen, the rainbow, Steven, the mask—the wholeness of it all, experienced all together, is what I'm calling the imaginal realm. So it's feeling our way into an ongoing awareness of our nesting-doll place in the world—as human beings in context. The word 'context,' of course, means 'with a text;' 'within a story.'"

"Because we're not objects in space," one of the dreamers offers. "We are not accidents alongside other accidents, or merely some kind of fallout from the Big Bang."

"We are ensouled beings who have a rightful place in the story," I nod. "And that place—our place—is being held for us by the world itself, by the Earth as an alive spiritual being, by *its* dream, and by all the images in it. If only we could open ourselves to the experience."

Then attempting to come at from a different angle, "What might it be like to be in touch with the things in your house? Really 'in touch?' As in, touching with your hands, your eyes, your heart? For what we discover when we touch things this way, is that these very same things become much more like living presences, like dream images, touching us in return. And together then, we are all touched into being. In other words, our touch touches these things and moves them into touching relationship with one another. So that the lamp over there and that table become 'friends.' And the entire room, filled with touching presences, now comes alive—much in the same way that dreams, and all the images in them, are alive during dreaming, which is precisely what makes the dream so attractive, because everything is all at once so alive and 'in touch.'

"And this is also why dreams spring to life again and again when we enter them on their touching terms, feeling our way along in the dark, rather than simply in terms of what they mean to us or for how we can apply them to our lives.

"The world is dreaming. So when we attend to the things of the world with the imaginal heart, through the mystery of touching, we are brought into intimate relationship with who and what we touch, and we are ourselves enlivened. Then the house stops acting like a museum and it becomes a living home.

"But I'd always thought that the presence of the human body, or of an animal's body for that matter, had everything to do with the soul-spirit-life in it. What became clear making the death mask is that the body's presence, its interiority—the very thing that makes it sacred—doesn't leave when the soul-spirit-life does. And I just never expected that."

"I'm curious," says someone in the group. "How did you know, or how do you know, that this is not just your psychic projection?"

"The interiority of the deceased's body? Or the making of the mask?"

"Either or both."

"Well, 'psychic projection' is a theory that assumes that we are all separate, isolated, closed in on ourselves . . . and so is everything around us. So, because we've consented to the divorce between thought and being, we have to invent 'mechanisms' to explain how we seem to be in connection. But our bodies don't know a dang thing about psychology. They know touch. They know being with and feeling through and reaching toward. They know relationship."

"But it could just be your projection, right?"

"It could," I concede. "But which is a better story? And if it is indeed a projection, then the mask had—and still has—as much a part in it as Karen and I do. In other words, the body of Karen's mother needed us to experience her sacred being in order for it to fully exist."

Then, "Look," I say, "Is this merely my 'bizarre imagination' as Sandy Meisner put it? Or are things like this happening all the time to everyone? And if so, well, then what? Are they merely going unnoticed? Are they being shrugged off? Ignored? Overwritten? Drowned out?" Then, "You've all heard the story of how my youngest, Jack, came into the world. Did I just make that up?"

JACK'S STORY

From across the hallway my three-year-old yells at the top of his lungs, "Dad?"

"He's not here, Jack," I call back.

"Where is he?"

"At work."

"Call him."

"Come snuggle."

Jack pads on over next to the bed and tries to pull himself up. I offer to help knowing that he won't take me up on it; he's at that age. He runs round to the end of the bed, clambers up the old school bench, and flings himself stuntman-like over the footboard onto the mattress. Then he scrambles up next to me and snuggles in.

I touch his peachy skin and play with his soft blond curls, winding them around my finger. He still smells like a baby.

"Can I still stay in your family, Mom?" he asks after awhile.

"Um-hum."

"Forever and ever?"

"Forever and ever."

Then, "Tell my story."

"Again?"

He nods.

"Okay," I say. "Are you ready for Jack's story?" He smiles. "It goes like this," I begin. "I was at a great gathering of friends. We had come together to celebrate my teacher's seventieth birthday, and Daddy was there, and Didier, who was only about ten days old. And I had just finished nursing your brother and was just putting him back in his little baby carrier, when I heard this voice say, 'Make me, make me, make me. I want to be part of your family.'

"I thought it was one of my friends playing a hoax on me so I swung around to see who it was, but there was no one there. I thought, 'That's strange. I could have sworn I heard someone.' And then I heard it again: 'Make me, make me, make me. I want to be part of your family.' So I swung round to look the other way; but there was no one there. Well, it was the oddest thing. I heard your voice loud and clear, calling to me from the Otherworld.

"I tried to tell myself that it was the voice of my unfinished schoolwork, but it wasn't very convincing. You just got louder. Finally, I could keep it a secret no longer. I went to your daddy and I told him what I was hearing. 'That's crazy,' he said, 'and anyway, what about my voice? What about what I want?'

"I said, 'I know, I thought we were through having kids, too. But I keep hearing this little guy saying, "Make me, make me, make me—I want to be part of your family." And I don't think there is much we can do about it except maybe make him.'

"Daddy said, 'No way.'

"I said, 'We have to at least try.'

"He said, 'Un-uh. Three's enough.'

"'Three is grand,' I agreed. 'But what about this voice I keep hearing? He won't leave me alone.'

"And your daddy said, 'He'll get over it.'

"But you didn't. You kept at me, and I kept at Daddy in turn. And then I got a notice in the mail saying that they were going to cut off my insurance at the end of the year. So if I was going to keep all the same doctors I'd had with your brother and sisters, we only had about three months in which to make you. I went to your father and conveyed my logic, but he wasn't moved by it.

"Later that same week the family was invited to a Winter Solstice party. We all went and had a wonderful time. That night, after the party was over and we were back home, I said to your daddy, 'Come on, why not at least try for three months? If nothing happens, well, we can say we honored the voice and we can send him back in search of a better family. It took us over a year to get pregnant with Marie-Claire, six months with

Esmé, and the same for Didier. It will probably take us longer than three months, but at least we'll be honoring the voice.'

"He said, 'I won't give you three months.'

"He'd never said 'no' like that before.

"'Three weeks?' I asked then.

"He shook his head.

"'Three nights?' I tried.

"'I'll give you one,' he held up his 'one' finger before leaving the room.

"Well, I started lighting all the candles immediately. 'Okay,' I whispered to you then, 'if I'm not making you up, and you really do want to be part of this family, now is your only chance.' And boom, wouldn't you know it, that's the night you came into our family, Jack."

"I almost didn't make it," Jack whispers then, his bottom lip beginning to quiver.

"But you did," I remind him. "You kept at me and I kept at your father and here you are. And now none of us can imagine our family without you in it. Daddy can't imagine it. Mommy can't imagine it. Your sisters and brother can't imagine it. Our family was not complete without you, Jack. But you were the only one who was wise enough to know that."

"I almost didn't make it," he says again, as if nothing I say has any impact on what he is experiencing.

"But you did, Jack," I repeat. "You did. Oh, it's a good thing you're so tenacious."

"I almost didn't make it."

"What's your real name?" I ask then, changing angles.

"Adjek Shaia," he answers.

"And what does it mean?"

He shrugs.

"Your name, Adjek Shaia, means 'the laughing gift,' Jack. *The laughing gift.*" He giggles and snuggles in closer to me.

"Can I stay in your family forever and ever, Mom?" he asks then.

"Forever and ever," I say.

"Thanks, Mom," he smiles.

"Thank *you*, Jack."

~~~~~

"How do we know what we know?" I ask those gathered. "How do we know *anything*? The dreamtime is forever trying to undo our small, stumbling ideas of what we think we know, or of what we don't know, and move us instead into our direct and connected knowing, into relational wisdom. We get caught, of course, conflating wisdom and information, but wisdom does not mean having all the right answers. Wisdom has everything to do with bodily knowing—with feeling our way along in living bodies. But we miss this altogether, or we don't trust it.

"We spend a great deal of time and energy trying to dissuade ourselves (and all those around us) that what's actually present is not present. It seems that this is because we've been taught, or perhaps conditioned, to do this. Or maybe it's because we have some puritanical idea of what we think ought be present, or what we want to be present, so we're busy trying to manifest it. But why are we not paying attention to what is actually present?

"Is it fear of the unknown and reacting out of that fear that keeps us in a closed system?"

"We live in constant fear of what could happen or of what might happen. Or of what has already happened and might happen again, or of what might not happen. So we are not really living in the present but are either stuck in patterns of the past or in a kind of perpetual fear of the future."

"Because which came first: the culture of fear or the insurance salesman?" someone asks rhetorically.

"So this is another thing that the dreamtime is always trying to do," I nod. "Or rather undo. The dreamtime is always endeavoring to move us from a closed system into an open one. So the rule with fear is this: instead of being afraid of what could happen, or of what might happen, we want to open ourselves up to what *is* happening," I say, taking a moment to let the group reflect on this. "For the work of love is always right before us."

Then, "What's happening right now, what's right before us . . . is that we're dangerously close to crowding out that whimpering bathroom creature," I let my eyes gently touch upon the dreamer who brought the dream creature in. "And we don't want to do that. So," I ask her quietly, "can you put yourself in that bathroom?"

She's there almost as soon as I make the request. "It just makes me so sad," she says, placing her hands over her face as she folds over in her seat. She lets out a breath-filled, anguished cry that sounds rather like a cat in heat, as she shifts her weight from side to side several times before returning herself to an upright position. "It makes me so sad. I don't think I can even talk about it," she says then, still shifting uncomfortably in her seat.

"We are not soul-making when we talk 'about' a dream," I reassure her. "We are soul-making when we talk 'with' a dream, alongside it in a companioning sort of way. You think you might be up for that?"

"It's that whimpering," she says, quietly assenting.

"Can you stay with it awhile? Allow it to penetrate?"

"It fills me with a kind of horror," she says after a time, "like, *what have I done?* It reminds me of that poem by Antonio Machado."

The Wind, One Brilliant Day

The Wind, one brilliant day, called
to my soul with an odor of jasmine.
"In return for my odor of jasmine,
I'd like all the odor of your roses."
"I have no roses; all the flowers
in my garden are dead."
"Well then, I'll take the withered petals
and the yellow leaves and the waters
of the fountain."
The wind left. And I wept. And I said,
"What have you done with the garden that was entrusted to you?"[10]

"That's it!" she says, reaching for the tissue box. Then, grabbing a couple of tissues, she dabs daintily at her eyes. "That's it exactly."

"Okay. But don't the Sufis remind us that forgetting is what it means to be human?"

"I know," she says. Then slapping her thigh, she lets out a frustrated, "Oh!"

"And that if we didn't forget we'd be God?"

"I know, I know," she says, yanking a couple more tissues from the box before blowing her nose.

"And so now you want to be reminded, too, of that old African proverb: the rain does not fall on your roof alone. We all forget. Good heavens, I teach the stuff and I forget! And yet each and every time we are remembered forward, we make the same vow: I will never, *ever* forget this again! But of course, 'cut to:' as they say in the film business. It's the stuff of comedy, the *Divine Comedy*, even. Humans are fallen creatures because we forever fall into forgetfulness. But take comfort in the fact that you are not being singled out. The whimpering creature and your forgetfulness of what's been entrusted to your care is the stuff of great poetry. And it's what moves you into Mystical Poverty."

"I know. I know. I know. I just . . ." she trails off.

"So now close your eyes and listen again to that whimpering. Can you hear it?"

She nods.

"Let the sound of the creature's helplessness move you into your own. Surrender knowing what to do, or even what to do next. For it's out of this condition, this not-knowing surrender that you can say to the creature . . ." I pause. "Well, let me ask you. What do you want to say to the creature?"

"You are there," she begins softly, "on the other side, even though I cannot see you." Then, "Thank you for coming to remind me of what I keep forgetting. I'm sorry, so truly and deeply sorry, that I've hurt you," she says, her voice cracking. "I want so much to promise you that I won't kick you any more," she pauses, "but all I can promise is that I will try."

This is when it's important to get very quiet, very still, for we want to let the dream unfold. We want to leave enough room, enough freedom of space, for the dreamer and the dream images to be just as they are for a time.

"Do you notice anything now?" I ask her some while later.

"It's as though the creature is my cat. It's not my cat, of course, but it feels like my cat even though I still cannot see it. Like a very large version of my cat, so completely innocent, and, though hurt by me, willing to forgive . . . to forgive me unconditionally."

"And what capacities of soul might you imagine you are being asked to develop in the presence of this once-hurt-by-you-and-now-unconditionally-forgiving creature?"

She shrugs. "Mindfulness?" she offers tentatively then.

"Okay. Mindfulness is good. What about a willingness to become a kind of attendant for the all-too-easily forgotten ones? A mindfulness for the hidden-from-plain-view ones who are desperate for our attention? The same ones that we all fear so much? Those ones that, when they take a step towards us, we kick and bite, scratch and scream at before we even know what they want from us?"

"Yes," she nods.

"Okay, good. Now you remember that very first dream you brought in here? It was some time ago," I prompt her.

"The one with the stray cat that was trying to get in my front door?"

"That's the one," I smile, as the same stray dream cat pads its way to the center of our circle. "And remember how I told you then that we would be looping back round to visit that dream over and over?"

"I remember," she nods.

"Well, we've just made another loop round. Another petal in the flower of your life has been rendered by the Artist. And so now I want you to do something along the lines of what you did then. Do you remember what that was?"

"I put a bowl of milk out each evening."

"In your not-knowing," I add. "Remember? You were to say, 'In my not knowing where this is going, I offer you this bowl of milk,' and then you were to set the imaginal bowl of milk on the floor as an offering, a gesture of gratitude for the images in the dreamtime. As a way to say, 'I see you'—even though in this particular case, of course, you do not see the bathroom creature at all— but you feel it. So it's a way to say 'I see the light in your being and I thank you for shining through me, through the light in my being. You are welcome to be with me. Now and always. Take this milk as a gesture of my thanks.'

"And as you set the bowl down you want to say, 'I have no idea where this is going. I set this bowl down for you, Whimpering Creature, in my not-knowing.'"

"I can do that," the dreamer smiles.

"Good. You'll also want to include that stray cat from your original dream. And," I pause, "the dream image that so horrified you a few months ago. The one of you slapping your cat."

She lets out a long and heavy sound as she slumps forward in her chair as if to say, *"Oh, why did you have to remind me of that?"*

"This is why we work with dreams communally," I say, looking around the room.

"Why do we do that?" someone asks, referring to the way we so easily fall into forgetting dreams, even dreams that are filled with images that have the power of penetration. "Are we trying to protect ourselves from knowing? Is it a defense?"

"Isn't it the nature of dreaming itself?" I ask. "Recall, if you will, the famous dictum of Heraclitus: *Nature loves to hide*," I pause. "Well, from what, might we imagine, does Nature love to hide?"

"From itself?" someone offers.

"Isn't dreaming the nature of soul expressing itself?" I suggest. "But it's a hidden, ineffable expression, and as such we are drawn deeper and deeper into the mysteries of the dreaming heart. If it weren't this way we could just read the backs of cereal boxes. Turn the dream over," I flip my hand over as though it's a cereal box, "to read its content label."

"Which is why those dream dictionaries are so altogether dissatisfying," someone offers then.

"Because there is no finding out what 'fox' means," the dreamer adds. "How can I possibly know what 'fox' means if I don't even know what 'I' mean?"

"'When at last we escape the barbed-wire enclosure of *Know-Thyself*,'" I say, reciting D.H. Lawrence, "'knowing we can never know, we can but touch, and wonder, and ponder . . .'" I pause. "So let them all be present," I say to the dreamer then. "All the cats and creatures. And what you'll find is that they're all trying to love you forward. But you've got to give them enough room to be present, enough room to move around, to cross in and out of the rooms and realms of the imaginal."

"Same bowl?" she asks then.

"Same bowl," I nod. "It's the gesture of doing this that matters, not the actual bowl and milk. So now do this every day for the next week, and then every few days over the course of the month between our gatherings. As a gesture. And we'll see what unfolds."

<hr/>

Dreams show us—even as we sleep and regardless of their particular contents—that we are creative beings. When we sleep we are returned to the source of our ongoing creation just as we are returned to ourselves as creative, ensouled beings. So every night is a holy night.

The line that we draw between the waking "real" and our sleeping, "Oh, it was only a dream," has more to do with the way we value one over the other. And this has everything to do with the current culture and its prejudice and preference of the ego's measurable experiences over and against those rather immeasurable experiences of the soul.

And isn't this also why, increasingly, the day world is encroaching upon the night world? Electrically lighting up the dark rather than allowing us to fall into it, and into sleep, so that we might make our way along the walls of the dark dreaming world as likewise lit-from-within, radiant beings of light.

Instead, over and over again the urge is to "understand" the dream—to look for the dream's meaning. But dream images don't mean anything—they simply *are*, just as we are. Dreams talk to some seed in us that *is*. What is the meaning of an iceberg? Of a fox? A whimpering creature? If we have to ask what it means, chances are we're not really seeing the iceberg at all, or we're not encountering the fox. We're not allowing the hurt and confusion of the whimpering to penetrate us, let alone getting still and curious enough to companion the creature.

What we discover when working this way is that dream images are not merely the projections of the dreamer. Rather they are autonomous images that appear in dreams in order to interact with us. It helps, then, to imagine that dreams are alive and that the images in dreams have lives and bodies of their own. However, not only do the images in dreams need our dreaming instruments and our embodied imaginations to be "dreamed" into being, it's also as though they require our unique participation in order to be fully present, to be fully embodied. Indeed, in order to make any "sense," they require our senses, especially our felt-sense, our intuition.

It also helps to think of dreams as community events—as a kind of town meeting of images, where each image has a life of its own, while still relating to the other images, including the dreamer. This is also why working with dreams in small dedicated groups is so valuable, because the work itself is a communal event—a kind of town meeting of people and images—where it's easy to experience the myriad ways that "image loves image" and "like cures like."

Dream images also want our contemplation. The word "contemplate," means "being within the temple," so it helps to imagine that we enter the temple of images with them. Once inside the temple, we practice staying open and radically receptive, becoming actively (and bodily—that is, through the senses) present to the images as they unfold, without losing a sense of who we are.

Gradually what we discover is that dreams are trying to teach us their way of thinking, of being. With practice and over time, this begins to directly influence our waking-world way of thinking and being. For one thing, thinking and being are no longer experienced as separate.

Slowly and surely we begin to discover that soul is in fact everywhere, and that the dream is happening now, and now, and now.

Part II:

Dreams as Initiation

This Fish Date

You pack your tackle
and head down to the water's edge,
to the spot we agreed on
by the undercut bank,
next to the downed tree,
while I swim around
trying to look as though
I'm not waiting for you.

I recognize your spinner
before it hits the water.
Black and gold,
with double reverse
blades through the shaft,
rotating
like a little aquatic insect
that I long to be lured by.

Then, as before,
you cast upstream
and let your spinner
drift with the current
gently
toward me.

I remember you mostly
with my mouth,
bleeding
sweetly,
as you pulled me ever so slowly,
across ages,
toward you.
Then, as you lifted
that long line from the water,

your storied hands
working firmly
against my wet skin,
fumbled
for the quickest release.

How did you know
that letting me go
would awaken
this ancient longing?

Dear One, this time
don't release me.
Uncrimp
your exquisite barbs
and keep me
within your limit.
Don't put me back in
with all the others,
this alive
and wanting to be
caught
only by you.

Take this knife.
Now,
angle it
toward the back
of my eye
and insert it
several times.
I will arch my back
momentarily
then go completely limp.
If I move
or try to whisper
anything to you after that,
you have not hit the right spot.
Try again.

My color should flood back
within seconds.

Sing those sweet songs then
as you drop me
into your waiting slurry
and carry me
to that first fish place
where once
we both were scaled and gutted,
cleaned, cooked, and eaten
by the One
who is ever dreaming us.

RUNNING TO HAPPY HEAD

"Dark feelers on? Heart ears open and venturing forth?" I funnel my
hand through the air in the shape of active listening. "Inner eyes peeled?"
Then, as everyone settles in, "There is a long part before this part of the
dream that I cannot remember," I begin.

Scads of dreams start with similar opening statements. And folks
tend to imagine that the details in the forgotten parts of the dream would
act as the "key" to understanding the remaining parts, if only they could
remember them. But it's actually not true. The fuzzy, forgotten parts
are how the dreamtime lets us in on the open secret that dreaming is
happening all the time.

"I'd been with a man named Happy Head," I continue, "but he had
to go home because he had something to do."

This is the set up of the dream, rather like what's referred to in the
film business as "the establishing shot"—the opening sequence of images
that establishes the general terrain and allows us to get a feel for things—
those first few, feeling-our-way-along-in-the-dark fingerfuls for what's
about to unfold.

"I'm in the kitchen of an old barn-shaped farmhouse that doesn't belong to me. Two people arrive—a big, brawny fellow and a woman who is not to be trusted—with the intent to take me away." I wrap my arms around my torso, straightjacket-style. "The sense is that it's to some kind of asylum," I say, fluttering my fingers next to my noggin.

"I know *immediately* that I don't want to go with them, so I run downstairs to the basement to get away. The woman and the muscle man then enlist the help of a mentally handicapped guy who lives in the place (and therefore knows it very well). And together they come after me.

"I have a large butcher knife," I indicate its size, "that I'm willing to use to protect myself. And now, I'm not sure how the couple knows this exactly . . . but they know that I won't hurt the handicapped guy because he's an innocent in all of this, and so they put him between me and them, knowing that I won't use the knife on him.

"So down in there in the basement, I'm looking around for a way out. I run into another room and think of digging my heels in, with my back against the door, because I know how incredibly strong I can be like this. But then I remember the size of that big brawny guy and I think better of it.

"That's when I notice a narrow, green door over on the left. And, as I pull the door open, light streams in from the outside. Then, as my eyes adjust to the light, I see a number of concrete steps—ten or twelve—that lead to the outside. I run up them as fast as I can.

"At the top, I don't hesitate. I start running and calling for Happy Head at the top of my lungs. 'Ha-ppppp-y Heeeeeead!' I cry out as I run cross-country through the surrounding farmland, past several out-buildings until, without any warning, I come upon a World Cup soccer match that's being played in a clearing. Happy Head and a few of his friends are watching the game from the veranda of Happy Head's house, which is on the far side of the clearing. I run straight for Happy Head, right through the middle of the World Cup match.

"Suddenly, I hear the sound of horse hooves beating down behind me and I turn to see the Woman Who Is Not To Be Trusted chasing me on horseback now! 'Happy Head! Happy Head!' I scream, trying desperately to reach Happy Head before the woman on horseback reaches me.

"I am running so fast that everything . . . slows . . . down," I slow my speech, imitating the slow-motion movement of time, as the geometry of being curves into swollen, pixelated waves and the space between things opens its durational doors to let some sort of slipping through take place.

"But just then I see that Happy Head sees me. Without the least amount of concern that I might not make it to him, he calmly moves down off of the veranda and over to a small clearing next to his house. Patiently and quite confidently then, he waits for me there.

"The horse is getting closer and closer," I place my right hand over my shoulder to indicate just how close. "Thick, hot horse breath and slobbering wet, foamy spume hit my shoulder, but I just keep running. I am running for my life.

"Then, as Happy Head opens his arms to welcome me, I collapse into them, sobbing with relief. His embrace is so comforting, so reaching through the ages," I make a thumbing motion over my right shoulder as though hitchhiking through several incarnations, "so eternal that . . . well, what I actually notice *most* about his embrace," I say carefully, then, "is a rather eerie stillness that Happy Head possesses—it's utterly serene—holy-and-human-at-the-same-time. *And it's something that I recognize, something that I remember.*

"The woman rides right past," I say then, lifting my arm as though it's the horse and rider riding by, "but she'll be back. I know that it's merely a matter of time, but I drop the knife to the ground anyway, for as long as I'm with Happy Head I know that I won't need it. Safe and held and deeply loved, I never want to leave Happy Head's eternal embrace.

"But then slowly it begins to dawn," I say in a halting, hazy, lint-filled way, "that this is a dream. And as I begin to move . . . actually as I am pulled toward the threshold of the waking-world by my body as it begins to wake, as if from the deepest sleep imaginable, the deepest sleep possible, I'm suddenly very aware of being in both worlds at the same time, again in that strange, depth-filled, swollen and pixelated, in-between, *is it or isn't it?* world. And it's as though I'm being physically torn from the arms of Happy Head's ancient and eternal embrace, like a statically charged sock being pulled from its mate upon taking them out from the dryer. And, in the deepest anguish imaginable, I sob deep, wracking sobs, for I do not want to leave Happy Head. Not now. Not ever. I wake up utterly devastated."

<hr />

After giving the images a chance to settle into the gathered listeners, "So, what strikes you?" I ask.

"I'm struck by the fairy-tale-ness of the dream," the woman next to me offers. "The way the whole thing unfolds as though it'll have a happily-ever-after ending . . . until you're pulled from Happy Head's arms and awakened."

"Me, too," someone adds. "And so it strikes me, therefore, as a dream of Spiritual Soul's awakening."

"Awakening an ancient longing that, until Happy Head's embrace, I wasn't even aware of," I say. "Yes." Then, "Anything else?"

"I'm struck by the couple that have come with plans to take you away," someone offers, "and the fact that it's these two specifically."

"What strikes you about them?"

"They strike me as feeling life that doesn't yet know how to think."

"Say more," I encourage her.

"Well, my husband gets mad at me all the time for this because, for example, we'll be driving in the car and he'll say something, and then I'll make some assumption about what he means based on what I feel when he says it, but I won't say anything. I won't turn to him and ask what he means. I'll just run with whatever I'm feeling. And then, oh, I don't know, ten or so minutes later, after I've run halfway around the world with whatever I'm feeling, I'll say something. And he'll be like, '*What?!*'" she swings her head around imitating her husband's reaction. Then, "'*Where the hell did that come from?*' And I can always trace it back to his earlier comment," she smiles and shakes her head.

"We feel it, therefore it must be true, even though we might be bringing it to the party."

"Like your son Jack's 'I-almost-didn't-make-it,'" someone adds.

"Along with a kind of secondary thinking, where we think 'about' what something 'means,'" I nod.

"When what I was feeling had nothing whatsoever to do with what my husband meant at all," she chuckles.

"So now can you all see the marvelous magic in an image that puts a woman who is not to be trusted and all brawn, no brains together? And the set-up is that something's not 'right' in my head," I add. "Now, I think my mother called me stupid only once. But, oh how it found its mark."

"Another one of those fated things?"

"Again like Jack's *I-almost-didn't-make-it*, though I'm sure my mother must've called my sister stupid, and my brother, too," I shrug. "Yet for whatever fated reasons 'stupid' didn't land on them the way it landed on me. So, in a sense, I'm always bringing 'stupid' to the party."

"But what if your mother never called you stupid?" someone else asks then, suddenly quite sullen. "I mean, my father called me stupid all the time and so . . ."

"Whoa! It's not because my mother called me stupid that I sometimes feel this way. Soul will have out. So soul is always looking for the right opportunities wherein we can receive the necessary and specific, that is, fated blows. So if 'stupid,' for example, didn't come this way— soul would've had to keep looking around for some other opportunity, for some erstwhile way, that I could be wounded precisely."

"But why should we have to be wounded at all? This way or any way?"

"The word 'bless' comes to us from the French *blessure*. It means 'to wound.'"

"So our blessings, so to speak, come out of our wounds."

"And when people talk about their feelings," I nod, "as in 'you hurt my feelings'—what might we imagine they're talking about?"

"Well, it seems to me that it's something to do with the threads we came in with."

"So, for example, with my son," I nod, "he gets essentially hurt, essentially offended whenever he finds himself in circumstances that highlight the 'I-almost-didn't-make-it' feelings he came in with. Even though, in a sense, he's always bringing this to the party."

He knows his story by heart, yet every time he hears it he has the same quiver-lip reaction. So hearing his story confirms for Jack what he came in with, that is, that he just scraped through. And, though he is hugely loved and tremendously valued within our family, Jack needs to experience and even suffer what it's like to be almost forgotten, not bothered with, or left behind."

"But why?"

"Well, for one thing, the natural soul loves drama. So when he cries and yells and behaves as though he is being left out, it is not because it is the truth per se, but rather because it's the truth that Jack came into the world with. So the things that hurt Jack's feelings are not the same things that, for example, hurt his brother's feelings or his sisters'. But isn't this because 'I-almost-didn't-make-it' is asking to be worked with through Jack? Isn't he trying to learn, from the inside out, his own value, so that, on a soul level, Jack can learn to not forget himself?" I pause. "Well, just like Jack, we all come in with stories, with natural soul circumstances wanting, needing, and ardently desiring to be worked with and through."

"So 'stupid' for you."

"Well, stupid is just an example, but yes. And yet no amount of schooling seems to change this feeling, which comes as a bit of a surprise," I chuckle. "And yet I'm intelligent enough to know that I'm not *really* stupid. I don't need any more advanced degrees to prove this to myself. So now isn't this feeling of stupid rather like that woman on horseback who is not to be trusted? The way it comes after me, the way it loops around?"

Regardless of what the natural soul feelings are for each of us, they make themselves known, that is, they highlight themselves and even assail us because they want something from us. So if we can learn to allow the feelings to be present, on horseback even, instead of somehow pretending that they're there not, or that we need to overcome them, or . . ."

"Trying to make things be otherwise," someone offers.

"It reminds me of that last line in that poem by Rainer Maria Rilke," one of the dreamers says. "'So take your well-disciplined strengths and stretch them between two opposing poles,'" she recites. "'For inside human beings is where God learns.'"

"'For inside human beings is where God learns,'" the woman next to me repeats slowly.

"It's this couple showing up to take me away," I continue then, "that actually reveals to me just how much I want and need and ardently desire to develop the natural soul. In effect, then, they set the natural soul of things in explicit dreaming motion. For it's through their presence and the looping around aspect of feeling stupid—among other unrefined natural soul feelings that I came in with—that I'm invited into discovering how just how smart, in fact, the feeling life is, or *can be*, when wrestled from the hands of the abstractors." I pause to let this penetrate. "So now, what else strikes you?"

"Happy Head," someone says. "I'm struck by Happy Head."

"What strikes you about him?"

"Everything," she shrugs. "Like, *who is he?*"

"He's the reason I'm generally reluctant to share this dream," I say, taking a deep breath, "because Happy Head has an ineffable, all-too-personal, theophanic quality that makes him terribly difficult—impossible, really—to convey. Even were I somehow able to convey the dream with all the riches of its images, with all of the emotions and the sensory experiences quite intact, indeed, even if a film could be made of the dream, or it could be downloaded," I mime unplugging a flash drive from my heart's drive and plugging it into an imaginal one in front of me, "there would be scant chance that you, or anyone, could enter the numinous, Holy Other quality that Happy Head evokes in me. Except, perhaps, through poetry," I add, as "Annunciation," that marvelous poem by Marie Howe, walks in the room:

> Even if I don't see it again – nor ever feel it
> I know it is – and that if once it hailed me
> it ever does –
>
> And so it is myself I want to turn in that direction
> not as towards a place, but it was a tilting
> within myself,
>
> as one turns a mirror to flash the light to where
> it isn't – I was blinded like that – and swam
> in what shone at me

only able to endure it by being no one and so
specifically myself I thought I'd die
from being loved like that.[11]

The room echoes in the silence carefully earned by the poet's words. Then, "'. . . *only able to endure it by being no one and so specifically myself I thought I'd die from being loved like that.*' When I first heard this poem it penetrated me instantly, as though it had been sent from Happy Head 'special delivery,' though, of course, I knew that the poet had penned it as part of a contemplative series on the life of Mary. With poetry, then, we might together participate in the *mysterium facinans*— which, though accomplished personally, that is, with specificity, and with precision, it somehow still finds its mark in our hearts."

"Mysterious faci . . . *what?*"

"Oh, because it's always what those guys do when they're trying to show us that something has a certain weighty significance," I say. "They bust out the Latin.

"Henry Corbin, for example, said that he had to resort to Latin when trying to find the right words to convey the *mundus imaginalis*, or the 'imaginal world,' because of that same problem we discussed earlier—the trouble, that is, with the word 'image.' But regardless of what it's named, he is nevertheless obliged to convey just what the imaginal realm is to us, to his readers.

"That said," I smile, "like those marvelous made-up words by Dr. Seuss—'Ooleck' and 'once-ler' and 'midwinter jicker,'" I cite a few examples. "Latin's a lot of tongue fun."

Then, "You'll find the term *mysterium tremendum et facinans*, which means 'fearful and fascinating mystery,' used a lot in the writings of Carl Jung and in the works of C.S. Lewis and Mircea Eliade.

"It was popularized by Rudolf Otto, a German theologian of the early twentieth century, along with the word 'numinous'—an adjective made by taking the Latin word *numen*—which means 'nod, divine sway, or divinity'—and tacking 'ous' on the end, so we end up with 'numinous,' a word that describes the presence and power of a divinity. In other words, it means getting a nod, so to speak, from the divine.

"Now Otto claimed that this 'nod from the divine' is experienced by us in two ways. The fear and trembling way, which is referred to as the *mysterium tremendum*. And the *mysterium fascinans*," I say, tilting my countenance heavenward while assuming a beatific expression, "or that which attracts, fascinates, and compels."

"In this way, Happy Head kind of reminds me of the third book of the *Divine Comedy*," one of dreamers offers then. "The first two books are so dark and twisted and yet still so accessible."

"Because they're so rich in imagery," someone adds.

"So we can easily go down into the underworld and vividly participate in everything that Dante encounters down there," she checks around the room to those who've read the books. "And in Purgatory, too. But by the time he gets to *Paradise*, it's all just *awhhhhhhhh*," she sings, placing her hand over her heart, "angels and bright lights, celestial spheres and whatnot."

"Celestial spheres and whatnot," I laugh, casting my eyes piously toward the ceiling. "Forgive them, dear Dante," I say then. "Yes, but Dante admits that the version of heaven he receives is one that his human eyes permit him to see. So the heaven that he conveys to us in the Cantos is the heaven that Dante is capable of. And if you look over there," I say, directing their collective attention to where the *Divine Comedy* sits on the bookcase, "what you'll notice is that there are many, many translations of *Hell*, only a few translations of *Purgatory*, and even fewer of *Paradise*—

for the very reason that you just mentioned, I suspect, because the translations either don't exist or they're not readily available.

"So as numinous experience goes, it seems that *mysterium tremendum* is more universally accessible, or perhaps more directly accessible, than *mysterium fascinans* because that which fascinates, attracts, and compels does so utterly personally, that is, with unique-to-the-individual specificity. And so yes," I turn to the woman who offered the comparison, "this is precisely the problem that I'm up against with Happy Head, which is not at all a problem between Happy Head and me. When it comes to conveying the experience to others, however, well, I suspect that Happy Head is never going to attract, or fascinate, or compel you toward him the way he does me. Yet the essence of the dream tells us that we're in numinous territory, in the presence and power of the divine that is at the same time initiatory.

"So, just as in the poem, when the dream originally occurred, the unequaled depth of love that I experienced in Happy Head's arms is so utterly stirring that '*I thought I'd die from being loved like that.*' And so, I gave up the life I'd been living. I gave up my marriage and career and I set off in solemn search of finding whatever ways I could imagine, discover, or divine—trying to make it back into those Most-Holy-and-Human arms."

"Did you feel like you had a choice in the matter?"

"I can clearly see the fated aspect of it, looking back. The dreamtime knew that I would take the dream very seriously, but it must also have known that I would take the dream rather literally. For how could it have been otherwise then? Remember, the dreamtime always puts us next to the River of Dreams precisely where and when we can cross. So the dreamtime understood that I had no way of knowing, or of behaving, differently. This, however, is a striking example of a dream image that is experienced as 'idol,' as something that I thought, indeed, *believed*, I could find 'out there' in the concrete world of things."

"And now you know you can't?"

"I *can*," I say. "And I think that I am, but not in the literal ways that I'd imagined. For the dream and the longing it evokes are meant to be the call."

"To what?"

"Being."

"Being what?"

"Not what, but who. It's a call into being 'no one' and 'so specifically myself that I thought I'd die from being loved like that,' because dreams are trying to remember us into being who we are really. So all dreams, and this dream especially because of the way it penetrates, are annunciations; they call us into being."

"Because they want something from us?" someone asks.

"Well, don't they?" I ask. "They certainly want our participation, for one thing. And our contemplation. But the call to being is going to be different, that is, unique, for each of us."

THE MYTH OF ER

There's an old idea—set forth by Plato at the end of his *Republic*—that each person enters the world "called." In the *Myth of Er*, Plato tells us that each soul is given a unique soul-companion—or *daimon*, as the Greeks called it—before being born. Together with this soul companion, then, each of us selects a particular image, or pattern, that we intend to live out on Earth, because, in Plato's view, souls are aimed. So it's with this specific goal in mind that each of us, with the help of the soul-companion, selects the best possible pattern—a pattern that has everything to do with what's trying to be worked through, soul-wise, during the course of our lives. Thus we select our parents, our bodies, our intellects, and indeed all of the fated circumstances of our lives.

In the process of arrival, however, we forget all that took place. We forget that we have been given soul-companions just as we forget that we have chosen a particular pattern or image to live out. And instead, we believe that we've come into this life empty—as clean slates. The task for each of us, then, is to remember what the soul saw while standing on the other side. What did we agree to come here to remember and display, to give the world for its sake?

"So is Happy Head your soul companion?"

"Well, the uneasiness I experience with saying who Happy Head is has everything to do with how readily we fall into the trap of literalism. No sooner do we hear Plato's *Myth of Er,* than we start sniffing around for our soul companions. But like all myths, the *Myth of Er* is just a story that's good to think with. Myths are stories that never happened but are *happening all the time*. In other words, myths—like dreams and like animals in creation stories—teach directly. So we don't need an elaborate psychological system to understand them because, not only is the experience direct, direct experience is what they're teaching.

"Therefore, what's true of Happy Head is actually true of all dream images. They draw us ever closer to the truth of who we are really, of who we're becoming. So, looping back round to your question, I have absolutely no idea who Happy Head is, other than Happy Head. I can, however, tell you what he brings me to, what he evokes, and so forth."

"What do you make of that name?" someone asks then.

"So embarrassing," I shake my head. "And thank heavens, right? For it's the kind of name that ensures I will never try to start my own religion of Happy Head," I laugh. "And yet what we don't want to miss is that he is named."

"You mean, at all?"

I nod. "Because it's another one of those distracting things to consider what the name 'Happy Head' means?" someone asks hesitantly.

"Well, who the heck knows what 'Happy Head' means?" Then, "Oh, sure, we might get curious and turn to *BabyNames dot com* in order to discover the various origins and translations that are commonly found in such places. And yes, perhaps names lead out or call forth some essential thread of being in us. My mother, for example, named me Nicole when I was born, but by the end of that first day she changed it to Renée. What did she see?" I shrug. "The name Nicole is nice enough. From the French, it means 'victory for the people,'" I smile. "The name Renée, also French, means 'reborn.' Now perhaps my life would have been exactly the same had I gone through it as Nicole. 'What's in a name?' asks young Juliet Capulet from her balcony."

"'A rose by any other name would smell as sweet,'" someone offers, finishing Juliet's most famous lines.

"Yet the 'reborn' quality of my life can hardly be denied," I continue. "How many near-death experiences can a body have before a fated, incarnational pattern of death and rebirth is firmly established and recognized? So perhaps it is worth considering if the dream might have penetrated any differently if Happy Head's name belonged to one of the established religious traditions—if, for example, his name was Krishna? Or Jesus? Or Siddhartha Gautama, the Buddha?" I pause.

"But now take a moment to reflect on some of your own dreams," I invite after a time. "And what you'll discover rather quickly is just how infrequently 'naming' actually occurs in the dreamtime. Though there are scores of folks—dream friends and familiars—we might consider 'companions' of the dreamtime—those we encounter night after night . . ."

"Some more intimately than others," the woman beside me grins, fluttering her eyebrows suggestively.

"Yet rarely, so rarely, do we ever know them by name," I continue. "We know them most usually by what they do, by their actions, or by one or another of their features, or some sort of quality or feeling they engender in us during the dream and afterwards. With Happy Head, however, what he does and what he evokes *are* his name."

"Okay, but with 'Happy' and 'Head,'" someone says, "and the fact that they're together, we have a fairly good, already formed, idea of what Happy Head means just by hearing it."

"Ah, very good," I acknowledge. "So we needn't engage in the secondary act of thinking 'about' what the name Happy Head means."

"Okay, so," one of the dreamers begins slowly, "is it how you go about getting a happy head?"

"When called upon during the dream, let's look at what Happy Head does," I suggest.

"He comforts, he consoles."

"Like the Paraclete," a woman across the way offers.

"A pair of what?" someone asks.

"Not a pair of anything," she chuckles. "The *Para-clete*. One who consoles or comforts, one who uplifts, or one who is called to intercede on our behalf."

"In the Gospel of John, Jesus says, 'I will ask the Father, and he will give you another Paraclete to be with you forever. He is the spirit of Truth whom the world cannot receive, for it does not see Him nor know Him, but you will know Him, for He is ever with you and will be in you.'

"And later in that same Gospel, Jesus says, 'Nevertheless I tell you the truth: it's to your advantage that I go away, for if I do not go away, The Paraclete will not come to you, but if I go, I will send him to you.'"

"Are you saying *Jesus* sent you Happy Head?" someone asks.

"I'm a mythologist," I laugh. "I'm not terribly concerned with having the Truth in a capitol 'T' kind of way—with possessing it, or even of knowing in full what it comprises. For what concerns us when we are working this way is a feeling toward truth that develops our attention—so it works to focus our minds along with the feeling life and the will. We feeeeeeeeel," I gently flutter my fingers, "our way into the truth of who we're becoming with the images, that is, through them—it's a tactile call into being, filled with nuance and subtlety."

Then, "So how does the truth live within the soul of each of us? And how does that truth express itself through our actions? Through our dreams? The truth is," I shrug then, "there's no way to know whence Happy Head came any more than we can know who he is, except perhaps to invoke the notion of *himma*."

"So Happy Head is created out of your . . ." she trails off.

"Love and longing," I finish her sentence. "Out of my ardent desire. So rather like the Barbie in that heart-shaped box when I was in the second grade. Love and imagination enter at the exact same moment. Remember *himma* develops the heart's ability to think. And it does this by expanding the heart's 'feeling-into' capacities to the point that Happy Head is directly experienced as utterly and essentially real," I pause. "But now Happy Head is created and experienced as utterly and essentially real out of my ardent desire . . . of what?

"Here is where we'll want to consider that other most important notion the Sufis have with regard to the imaginal—*ta'wil*. For *ta'wil* ostensibly charges us with the task of carrying sensible forms back to their imaginative beginnings. When we do this, the images themselves take on a higher meaning.

"So with *ta'wil* in mind, we want to feel our way slowly into the image of Happy Head and notice what we notice. And one thing we notice, actually rather quickly, is that the image of the Paraclete in the myth of Jesus and the image of Happy Head seem to like each other. That is, they have a certain 'sympathy of being,' a resonance."

"The *myth* of Jesus?" someone suddenly exclaims.

"Not in the pejorative sense," I mutter. "Joseph Campbell, that late great mythologist of the last century, teaches us that one person's religion is another's mythology, and vice-versa. So some folks will no doubt be offended when they hear Jesus referred to mythologically rather than, say, historically or theologically," I shrug.

"On the other end of the spectrum, there are those who shun anything and everything having to do with Jesus because of the already established religious implications. What does Henry Corbin call this?" I smile. "'The agnostic reflex.' But aren't both ends of the spectrum suffering from impoverished imaginations? From narrow literalisms that tend toward fundamentalism?" Then, "The Jesus that concerns us here, however, has everything to do with initiatory experience."

"Regardless of whether one is a believer or not?"

"Belief has very little to do with finding one's place in an initiatory story. Or in any story, for that matter, unless it's trying to undo our beliefs about the way things are, especially our all-too-narrow beliefs about ourselves and about how the world works.

"Why is it that we can hear myths from the Hindu tradition, for example, and find our place in any one of those stories quite easily without troubling ourselves over whether or not we believe in the fantastic gods and goddesses included therein? A god with an elephant head! Why, the myths themselves keep us from taking them so literally."

"So the dreamtime is unconcerned with whether or not someone is a baptized Christian, for example?"

"Or even a Believer," I nod. "A propitiating Hindu, or a Buddhist who's taken refuge. These are just the details. The kinds of surface specifics that, though we are terribly taken with them, that is, by them, the dreamtime is fundamentally unconcerned with."

"Why the Jesus story at all?" a fellow across the room pipes up. "I mean," he shrugs, "why not a Ganesh myth?"

"Oh, there are plenty of those. We've all had dreams with animals that didn't make it onto the ark, have we not? I work with a guy, for example, whose dreams are filled with all sorts of fantastic, stitched-together amalgam animals. This one's a donkey with droopy, dangling, elephant ears. And that one's a polar bear with the neck of a giraffe."

"But these aren't . . ." he stops himself. "How are these Ganesh dreams?"

"Amalgam animals—or those creatures that did not make it onto the ark—act as Ganesh in his 'Remover of Obstacles' capacity in dreams, in that they help to remove the obstacle of our literal way of thinking. It's not by accident, therefore, that the 'Remover of Obstacles' is also 'Lord of the Beginnings.'"

"So we need to remove our literal ways of thinking when beginning anything."

"And especially with the kind of engagement we're after here with images," I add.

"Just the other day, a dream of mine featured big . . . very big . . . giant, in fact . . . shiny blue-black ravens with deep, pelican-like beaks," someone offers.

"*Ravicans*," the woman beside her says, naming the dream creatures.

"*Pelicavens*," the dreamer snorts.

"What's important to recognize about these creatures is that they're mythological. So it's not so much what the pelicavens are. It's what they're doing—how and when they're doing it, and with whom."

"They're moving monkeys," the dreamer blurts out, "from one see-through, leafless tree to another, in their big, black, pouch-y, pelican-like beaks. And the monkeys are like, 'Whoa!' It scares the hell out of them," she says. "But then one of the monkeys jumps off the tree onto my husband's back. And he's like . . ." she mimes wrestling a monkey that's on her back. "And no matter what he tries, he just can't get it off," she looks over at me then. "It made me think of a 'monkey-on-your-back,' you know, as in addiction."

"During the dream?"

"No," she shakes her head, "afterwards, upon reflection. During the dream, I'm just busy watching everything that's going on."

"Then what happens?"

"Wait!" someone interrupts. "I don't want to lose the thread of Happy Head."

"Oh, it's right here," I assure her, as I pull an imaginal, dreaming thread from my heart, wind it around my ring finger, and tie it into a knot. "We have a choice, of course, but . . . the monkeys are already in the room."

"On our backs now," someone adds.

"And there's no way to get them off, if, in fact, that's what we're going to do, except by following the dream to see what unfolds."

However, the woman who hollered 'wait!' is visibly disappointed by this sudden turn of events.

"What is this except the dream of the whole thing unfolding?" I ask then. "It doesn't make much sense, especially up on the surface of things. But if we endeavor to meet dreams down and around and just so, where they are, perhaps then we can begin to experience the marks of their indelible dreaming magic? The only way through what's actually presenting, is through the dream of the whole thing, which includes the Happy Head dream and now . . . the pelicaven dream. It includes even our resistances and the certain displeasure we sometimes experience with the way things go, or appear to be going. But we'll come back to

Happy Head," I reassure her. "Now then," I say, turning to the pelicaven dreamer, "go on."

"Well, with great effort, my husband finally manages to get the monkey off," she continues, "but no sooner does he do this than it jumps right on his back again!"

"Same monkey?"

"And the struggle continues," she nods. Much to our amusement then, she mimes a comical, many-armed-and-legged wrestling match between her husband and the monkey, with the monkey appearing as though he'll remain the undefeated champion.

"Whenever anything is doubled up in the dreamtime," I remind everyone, "it's trying to get our attention."

"So twice this happens before my husband just sort of loses it. And without thinking too much, I guess, and still trying to get that monkey off, he just plunges himself into the pool. And, though he manages to free himself from the monkey, he inadvertently catches his thumb," she holds up her left thumb, bending it a few times for added visual emphasis, "on the side of the pool. And it almost takes his thumb off," she says then, not bothering to hide her annoyance. "So then he comes up from the water . . . and . . . there's blood . . . everywhere. And his thumb is just hanging there then by the smallest of fleshy threads . . ." she lets out a deep sigh.

"And where are you during all of this?"

"I'm standing over closer to the house—which is my in-laws' house."

"Your in-laws' house."

"Well, not really, but that's the felt-sense."

"Okay. So, Place-of-In-Laws-Dreaming. And the camera?" I ask then. "Where is it?"

"My eyes. It's all my perspective, my POV—the whole dream. And all I can think is about how tired I am, how late it is, and how I just want to go home," she sighs. "But now my husband has gone and ripped his thumb almost clear off! So I know I'm going to have to spend the rest of the night in the emergency ward of the local hospital. And I know I should be all concerned for my husband and everything, and his thumb, but I'm like, '*Awwww, crud!*'"

"And that's where the dream ends?"

"That's where the dream ends," she confirms. Then, suddenly remembering, "Oh, but our son is like, 'Whoa Dad, are you okay?' he says, stepping toward his dad and looking at his thumb as though it's some kind of radical science experiment."

"The coolest thing he ever saw?"

"Yeah," she makes a face. "And that's where the dream ends. With our son stepping toward my husband, blood everywhere and my husband's thumb just dangling there, and with me being tired, fed up, and pretty ticked off."

"Okay, so sticking with our theme of mythological animals trying to move us out of literal thinking while at the same time trying to focus our attention specifically," I say, "what might you imagine they're trying to get you to see here?"

"I have a fairly strong felt sense that it has to do with the addictions," she says, "but other that that, I have no clue. Though I do feel pretty badly about not being more concerned with my husband's thumb."

"Did you feel badly about that in the dream? During it?"

"Well, I don't think it's near as fascinating as our son does, that's for damn sure!" she snorts. "I think that I should be somewhat more concerned for my husband, but all I can think about, really, is how stupid it was for him to plunge into the pool without thinking, how tired I am, and how I don't want to spend the entire night in the emergency room."

"Fair enough," I say. "So you don't feel particularly concerned for your husband and his ripped-off thumb during the dream."

She wads her facial features into a crumpled ball. "His *mostly* ripped-off thumb," she modifies.

"So, in other words, the doctors can reattach it?"

"Yeah," she says. "And, oh, sure it's bound to be an ordeal for my husband and everything, but it's salvageable, so I'm like . . ." she shrugs. Then, "I feel kind of badly about that. Especially when I hear you say it, when I hear it back like that," she adds. "But that's the truth of it."

"Well, the truth is what we're after," I reassure her. "So don't worry about the dream in terms of being 'The Indifferent Wife' or whatever it is that you're imaging it's saying about you in the waking-world. This would be to take the dream literally and we don't want that."

She laughs with relief.

"These are not the sorts of things that concern the dreamtime, though perhaps I should also add here that the dreamtime is not terribly concerned with giving us any relief from what it means to be human either. In fact," I stress, "on the contrary."

"Why did you ask where the camera is?" asks someone then. "Is it because it's where the action is? The energy and focus?"

"Well, that's the wholeness of the dream taken all together," I say. "Yet despite what appears to be the dramatic action in the dream, the concentrated touching between the dream and the dreamer takes place where the camera is. The camera therefore acts as a kind of 'lens of the heart,' focusing the place of the dream's penetration precisely.

"So how might the small, tenderized opening that's here, with the tiniest bit of crumbling around the dreamer's apparent lack of concern for her husband and his mostly ripped-off thumb, be allowed to do its penetrating work? For it's this wee opening that will perhaps allow us a way in, in order that we might see what's actually there."

"So it's not what happens to her husband?" someone asks.

"Well, they're the same thing," I say. "But the way into what's happening with her husband—which throughout the dream remains, in a sense, 'over there,'—is through this small place where the dream endeavors to touch the dreamer into being. So what's over there, where her husband is, and what's right here, where she is—that is, as the 'dreaming-I'—might be experienced wholly and simultaneously by the dreamer."

"So . . ." the dreamer pauses, not sure of how to proceed.

"So let's get curious," I suggest. "What do those pelicavens do?"

"They move monkeys," she gapes her mouth as though forming a pelican beak, "in their mouths, from one leafless tree to another. Though they're not trees that have lost their leaves. They're always leafless. Like something out of a Tim Burton movie."

"So they're dreaming, mythological trees?"

"Like the birds," she nods, "who are the only ones who meet with any monkey-moving success."

"Well, your husband gets the monkey off his back eventually," someone on the other side of the room offers.

"But not without a cost," the dreamer adds, bending her left thumb again for display.

"Weirdly, what happens with your husband's thumb makes me think of Ganesh," someone else pipes up. "Maybe it's because Ganesh is already in the room," he shrugs. "But his earliest name, for those of you who may not know, is Ekadanta. It means 'One-Tusked,' and it refers to the sacrifice that is necessary to complete any accepted task. Because Ganesh himself broke away his own tusk," he mimes breaking off a tusk, "so that he could use it as a writing implement in order to complete the *Mahabharata* as it was being dictated to him."

"So getting monkeys off your back requires a blood sacrifice?" someone asks.

"The word 'sacrifice' means 'sacred offering,'" I add. "But why are the birds in this dream necessary then? In other words, if this is what the dream is trying to show us—and we have to imagine that at least it's trying to show us this much—why are pelicavens in the dream at all?" I pause. "Why have they come to visit? Surely we could get this idea directly, just by what unfolds between her husband and the monkey. So why those birds?"

"Because no image is a throwaway," someone offers as a general reminder to everyone, while pondering the puzzle of the pelicavens.

"Even if there were such things as throwaways," responds the dreamer, "these particular birds, the pelicavens, would not at all be the sorts of images that would qualify. And not just because they're so big and weird, dark and otherworldly," she says then. "They scare the living daylights out of that monkey! He's filled with all kinds of new respect for pelicavens after that. They're effective at moving the monkeys in a way that my husband is not. And so . . . it strikes me that the only way to move the addiction monkeys is . . . *mythologically*."

"Because no amount of wrestling works. Every time your husband finally gets one of those monkeys off his back, it just jumps right back on."

"And it keeps happening until he does something stupid," she nods.

"Out of desperation."

"Yes," she half-heartedly agrees, "but with fallout for all those around him. Or at least for me," she corrects herself then. "Our son doesn't seem to be terribly troubled by it all."

"He seems attracted by it," someone offers, with what seems like a hint of warning. "Drawn in, even."

"Ah, but now remember, it's not really her son any more than it's her husband," I caution. "They're both asleep in their beds, just as is our dreamer. So 'dreaming-I'—the image the dreamer readily identifies as herself in the dream—is all that she knows and already recognizes about herself, however dimly."

"So it's a dreaming-ego image?" someone asks, as several of those gathered trail off into a bramble of confusion.

"The dreamtime uses her husband and her son as dreaming stand-ins," I say then, at the risk of becoming the village explainer, "cleverly, and oh, so specifically, intelligently, that is, with imaginal intelligence—so that she might relate to these aspects of being. In other words, so that she is able to see these aspects of being outside of herself. Just as it is for all of us, right?

"We can see the stuff on someone else but we just can't see it on ourselves. But now remember Rumi says that whatever we really see, well, that's what we are. The problem we generally have, however, with seeing it on others is that we get too caught up in the surface details. But now the task we are always charged with, according to the Sufis, is to turn the heart mirror around to ask: 'Okay, but now how *am* I like that?' And then listening, deep listening, as Rumi says,

> What is the deep listening?
> Sama is a greeting
> from the secret ones inside the heart,
> a letter.
>
> The branches of your intelligence
> grow new leaves
> in the wind of this listening.
> The body reaches a peace.
>
> Rooster sound comes
> reminding you of your love for dawn.

The reed flute and the singer's lips:
the knack of how spirit breathes into us
becomes as simple and ordinary as
eating and drinking.

The dead rise
with the pleasure of listening.

If someone can't hear a trumpet melody,
sprinkle dirt on his head
and declare him dead.

Listen, and feel the beauty of your separation,
the unsayable absence.

There's a moon inside every human being.
Learn to be companions with it.
Give more of your life to this listening.

As brightness is to time, so you are to
the one who talks to the deep ear in
your chest.

I should sell my tongue and buy a thousand ears
when that one steps near and begins to speak.

I should sell my tongue and buy a thousand ears
when that one steps near.[12]

"Sama is the whirling ecstatic prayer that Rumi initiated into the
world. And that 'moon inside every human being' is the heart-mirror. It's
the central image the Sufis have for what makes us uniquely human. And,
according to the Sufis then, as humans we are always charged with the
task of ever polishing our heart mirrors, with cleaning and shining them,
and with reflecting, that is, with using them to see what's 'out there' and
then turning the mirror round to see not *if* it's in here inside of us but *how*
it is here inside of us."

"Because it's all inside?"

"Henry Corbin calls this practice of polishing our heart mirrors and turning them around 'perpetual hermeneutics'—which, as he suggests, is the unending task of interpreting ourselves and the world around us so that we don't fall prey to dogmatic certainties and the delusion of absolute knowledge.

"In other words, there is a straight-up correlation between the sort of spiritual journey that's being advocated here and the psychological process commonly known as 'withdrawing projections.' Thus, as dreaming lovers of wisdom, we are charged with the task of discovering these projections and thereby beginning the long, slow, and often agonizing process of unveiling ourselves and the other at the same time.

"'Projections' are another way of saying 'idols,' and not because we worship them, exactly, but because we assume that they are true. This is because they seem so true, so powerful, so obvious, and so objective. But they are not, of course, because they come from us. And yet, they don't only come from us. There is also an element that comes to our eye from that which we are seeing. And this is what makes the unveiling work so fraught. Yet it is also precisely where we can move through the portal that the *vesica piscis* provides, so that we might begin to see, that is, really see, what is actually there, so that we might successfully render what has hitherto been experienced by us as an 'idol' into an 'icon.'

"The process of coming to understand that these apparent certainties about the world and others we know, or think we know, in fact belong to us and originate in our own psyche, is one of the most difficult in human experience. It is the slow work of many years.

"Note, however, that this 'moon' inside every human being that Rumi invites us to become companions with is not a head mirror; it's located inside the chest. So it's not a matter of thinking 'about' what we see 'over there,' as it were. Rather, it concerns feeling our way into these kinds of soul encounters that are at once 'over there' and 'in here.'"

"So," the dreamer hesitates, "are you saying then that dreams are all that we recognize about ourselves put into a larger context of all we don't recognize about ourselves?"

"In a nutshell. Though we should add that dreams are all we don't recognize about ourselves *and the world*," I emphasize. "We're embedded beings, so we've a rightful place in the world. We're being held in a nesting-doll place. But because we only ever know what it feels like to be us on the inside, we all too often take what it feels like to be us on the inside as the whole picture.

"So when, for example, Gertrude Stein says that each of us is only ever one age on the inside, consider how this is true. Every year we put another candle on the birthday cake. And yet, don't we more or less feel the same age on the inside throughout our lives? Heck, I still feel twelve or thirteen! Which explains why I'm drawn to doing mask work with kids this age."

"Because in some ways you've never left the sixth grade?"

"Precisely. But now when those same sixth-graders look at me they're not seeing the twelve- or thirteen-year-old that I feel myself to be on the inside. I'm the middle-aged mask lady to them."

"It's just like when we hear our voices on a recorder," someone across the room offers then. "It's never not shocking. We turn to our friends and ask, 'Do I really sound like that?' And when they say 'Yeah,' we don't believe them," she shakes her head. "I never seem to get over how strange my voice sounds coming from a recorder."

"And there must be all sorts of physiological reasons for the differences in the way that we hear ourselves from the inside and the way we hear ourselves from the outside. Nonetheless, it's a good way of opening up that what it feels like to be us on the inside is only a small part of what it means to be us really. And this is another one of the things that the dreamtime is always endeavoring to open up for us."

"Okay," the dreamer clears her throat. "I can see that my husband has done something stupid with regard to the monkey on his back, and God only knows that I've been there," she admits. " But why do I need to see my son's fascination with it? Is this, as was intimated," she looks across the room, "a warning?"

"Well, in the sense that Carl Jung says that whatever we do not meet in the unconscious will be thrust upon us as a circumstance of fate, yes," I answer. "But this is true of all dream images. So, it's not a warning about the dangers of addiction for your son. The dreamtime is not so crude," I shake my head, "not nearly so crude. Not Ever. No," I say then, slowly rocking my head from side to side, as though earthworming deeper and deeper into the dirt of the dark, dreaming underworld, "it seems that this is perhaps an attempt to highlight how you're not really there."

"You mean because I'm already in the emergency room?" she says suddenly. "Because I'm fantasizing about being up all night, having to drive all the way home afterwards, and thinking about just how tired I'm going to be at work tomorrow?"

"And kids your son's age don't generally do this. They're mostly in the moment."

"Which is why we're always having to teach them to think of the implications of this or the ramifications of that," someone adds. "All that frontal lobe stuff that takes so long to develop."

"Precisely why car-rental companies won't rent to anyone under the age of twenty-five," I smile.

"But I'm always in the future," the dreamer says then. "Fearing what could happen or what might happen. Like I'm playing chess in my head and strategizing my next five or six possible moves."

"That's the future as feared fantasy, not the future as it's actually unfolding now and now and now."

"So the best way to move anything with regard to the addiction monkeys is to stay in the present?"

"Well, 'staying in the present' is too abstract," I suggest. "Furthermore, if you notice the way the dream unfolds, what you'll want to consider is how the addictions, that is, as you practice them specifically, are perhaps your attempts to get bodily out of the present. In other words, out of the direct experiencing realm."

"Whoa!" she says, as though some notorious nail has just been hit on the head. Then, "That's why I took up yoga!" she blurts out. "I had to find a way to be in my body and feeling, experiencing. Anything!"

"Wait," someone asks. "You're not suggesting that yoga is her addiction are you?"

"Well, it could be but . . ."

"Yoga's what I do in answer to the addictions," the dreamer interjects.

It's important to wait here, to pause just long enough to give the feeling connections between the dream images and the dreamer a place to be.

"Okay, so now let's get curious about these mythological birds," I suggest after enough time has passed. "What do you make of them?"

"Well, monkeys fear them," she laughs. "But ravens are both above- and below-world creatures. And pelicans go below the water to fish in those big, pouch-y beaks of theirs. So it seems to suggest that pelicavens have access to more than one world, more than one realm. So . . . it's a more-than-one-realmed approach that perhaps has the best chance at moving the addiction monkeys," she suggests.

"A more-than-one-realmed approach," I repeat slowly. "So might this suggest that, for example, it's not just the physical body in terms of what it can do in yoga, that is, position-wise?"

"Yoga is a discipline that's concerned with the physical, the mental, *and* the spiritual," she emphasizes. "And the kind of yoga I practice focuses on the purification of the body, which, in turn, is supposed to lead to the purification of the mind, and to 'prana,' or vital energy."

"Uh-huh," I say. "And is it?"

"You mean, doing that?" she asks.

I nod.

"Yes," she says. "I mean, I think. While I'm doing it anyway. Then I am most genuinely, most authentically, most really and truly aligned with myself. But the rest of the time," she shakes her head, "I'm so frantically busy. I work full time and when I'm not working, I'm doing stuff for the family, cooking or doing laundry, running errands, driving the kids to their games, and . . . when all of that is finally done, or I've done all that I can do in a given day, all I want to do is unwind with a glass of wine— take some much needed 'me' time—but then the next thing I know, it's time for bed," she throws her hands in the air and lets them fall to her thighs with a sudden slap. "I go to bed feeling guilty for all that I didn't get done. And I wake up feeling exhausted, only to start the day, and the cycle, all over again," she says. Then, "Sometimes it just makes me want to run away and join the circus," she snorts.

"Does this sound familiar to any of you?" I ask casually, as the room groans loud and long and theatrically.

"It's like I don't know who I am without all that I do," says someone across the room, as she jumps from her seat and stands with her arms stretched akimbo. "I'm so completely identified with 'the Accomplisher.'" Then, "Dum, dah, dah, dahhhhhh," she sings, thrusting her chest heroically forward. "Like one of those giant Macy's Day Parade balloons," she slumps back down to her seat. "And . . . I don't know how else to be."

"Well, what is this except the monkey on our cultural back?"

"You mean, we're addicted to doing?" the dreamer asks.

"Well, perhaps 'addicted' is too strong a word," I suggest. "But, aren't we? What is all this frantic running around if the not the 'clamor of our metaphysical distress,' as Mir Damad puts it?"

"Remember a few years ago," the dreamer says then, lowering her voice while narrowing her eyes, "when one of those balloons—the Cat-in-the-Hat, I think it was—came loose from its moorings? And it floated through the streets of Manhattan terrorizing all of the parade-goers? You think, balloon . . ." she shrugs, "how bad can it be? But then it almost kills a few people!"

"That's what it feels like," says the Accomplisher, "when I'm doing too much—like I might actually kill a few people if I'm not careful," she almost laughs, then, "Really. Like I might career out of control."

"Isn't this why so many car accidents take place within the two-mile radius of where we live?" one of the dreamers offers then. "Because in those last two miles we're already home in our minds—thinking about doing the laundry, or putting the groceries away and 'What should I make for supper?'" she says then. "So we're not where we are and we're not doing what we're doing; we're off somewhere already onto the 'next' thing."

"Or then I'm deflated," the Accomplisher adds. "As if the helium or whatever's keeping me afloat and accomplishing is wearing off. So I'm constantly on the lookout for more things to do, hoping that one of them will be exciting—and that it might actually give me more energy."

"Which brings us around to: why the thumb?" I ask.

"You mean, as opposed to the head or . . ."

"As *opposed* to," someone pipes up. "Oh, no pun intended!"

"Some other part," I chuckle. Then, "Yes. What do you make of that thumb?"

"Well, it's opposable," she nods to the punster.

"It's what separates us, actually, from the monkeys," someone across the room adds, rotating his thumb round while padding his fingers with it for emphasis. "So it's a true pulp-to-pulp opposition. It's how human beings are actually able to do all that we can do."

"And yet we know that the dreamtime isn't terribly concerned with what we do. And that it's even less concerned with the amount that we're doing," I say. "These are just the details. However, the dreamtime *does* seem to show a good deal of interest in how we do what we're already doing, with how we do anything."

The Myth of Efficiency

At the risk of making mythologists everywhere cringe, the word "myth" in the pejorative sense seems rather fitting here. So just what is the myth of efficiency? Well, it goes like this. We tell ourselves that if we can just get through these dishes and fold that pile of laundry, *then* we'll get to unwind with a glass of wine, or watch our favorite programs, or do that thing, finally, that we really want to do—yoga, or whatever. But any time we are working just to get the thing off of our proverbial plates, so to speak, in a quick and efficient way so that we can then get to do the thing that we really want to be doing, we've fallen out of soul. For as Robert Sardello reminds us, body and soul are equal; so any time we put the needs of one before the other, even for a moment, we've fallen out of soul.

"Is there a way to be 'in soul' while doing the dishes or mopping the floor or any everyday thing?" the dreamer asks.

"It first involves re-animating the world," I nod. "So that the world, the Earth, and everything in it—including the hidden-from-plain-view things and all that's more vividly displayed—is approached with reverence and wonder, and with devotion and surrender. Everything.

That is, not just the cute fuzzy things that make us all go 'awww,' but wrestling, won't-leave-us-alone monkeys too, and pelicavens, and see-through Tim Burton trees, the Happy Heads, and those Shes-who-are-not-to-be-trusted, as well as the all-brawn, no-brains beings that accompany them, the stray cats and the sad slaps and all the whimpering creatures, iceberg tips and the larger parts below, that, though they remain mostly hidden, are nevertheless uniquely capable of sinking our Titanism. And all those things in the world that seem to be happening 'over there.'

"Because everything, as Mir Damad reminds us, is a twofold being; everything in creation has nothing in itself and indeed *is* nothing in itself. So everything has both a side we see and a side we don't see, a side we know and a side we don't know, including us. And what this reveals to us, again, is our Mystical Poverty.

"Thus, if we can begin to surrender to the enduring and unbreakable unity of these two sides of creation—which by necessity means that we are required to move out of a closed system and into an open one— we can begin to feel our way into the awe and mystery and animation of all the things of the world, until everything—the Earth and all her phenomena—is reanimated, brought back to life like Lazarus, so that the Earth is no longer reduced to something we merely live on, that is, *off of.*

"But this requires that we, too, must be brought back to life. We too will want to re-animate into living bodies, so that our bodies are not just things that we are living off of. For isn't that, in effect, what we're doing? Living off of our bodies? Don't we prize our bodies when we can get them to do what we want? And forget about them, neglect or even revile them when they behave badly? Or when they fall into symptom and don't function 'accordingly'? Or when they don't live up to our expectations of them? Don't we rate them depending on how well they're performing? Or on how good they look? How young, how slender, or how good they are in bed? Or perhaps we become overly concerned for our bodily comfort . . . pampering our bodies as if they are our pets. Don't we consider them 'ours,' that is, as something we have ownership of? And don't we imagine therefore that we can do whatever we want to do with them, or to them? Or not? It's uncanny how what we're doing to ourselves we're also doing to Earth—but how could it be otherwise? If we're not living relationally within our own bodies, how could we expect to be living relationally within Earth?

"So how might we accept the ongoing invitation of Mystical Poverty and begin to encounter the Earth and all her phenomena as beings? Is there a way to experience one another in our authentic existence, that is, directly, without any qualification or objectification? Even, or perhaps especially, with those people who we think we know, including ourselves? Is there a way to suspend what we think we know, so that we might feel our way into discovering one another, moment by moment, image by image? Is there a way to approach the very world we live in, and all the things in it, right here, right now, including the dirty dishes and the floors that need mopping, as though they're beings with a material, plain-view aspect and an immaterial, but nevertheless essential, hidden-from-plain-view aspect that likewise evokes our own hidden-from-plain-view-ness? Can we come deeper and deeper into discovering our nesting-doll place in the world just by participating in it, that is, with it, image by image, encounter by encounter, so that whatever we engage in becomes included in the equation of what we came here to remember and display?"

"As if everything's a yoga practice," the dreamer nods.

"So that you're . . . how did you put it?—'most really and truly aligned' with yourself and in the world," I say, "that is, with the world, aligned with Earth and her spiritual soul's unfolding."

"And not just when I'm folding myself into yoga positions on a mat somewhere," she offers.

"So we practice our lives and everything in them," someone offers.

"As lovers of Earth and the imaginal world. As if the whole thing's a dream that we're weaving ourselves into. Or perhaps it's merely a practice of noticing, in an ongoing way, how we're already woven into the dream of things, and noticing then how that weaving continues and how it's influenced by our heart-felt willingness to participate in it."

"So then . . ." the dreamer hesitates, "there's really no such thing as 'me' time. That is, separate and over there and throwing my hands in the air because I haven't had a moment of time to myself . . ."

"Everything is a form of 'me' time if this same 'me' time is for the sake of the Angel of our Being, that is, if we are oriented toward the Angel so that literal realities are seen from within. But, as this is not an ego activity, the world does not get internalized into me. Instead, what we soon discover is that we are turning inside out into the world in such a way that what once was experienced by us as 'over there' is happening 'in here' now and now and now."

"Can you give us a concrete example?" someone asks then.

"Let's take some otherwise mundane thing like 'sweeping,' something that doesn't require our intense concentration so that we are freed to be relaxed with what we are doing. So we can stay 'on task' and still be freed up enough to ask another one of the central questions of creative imaginal work, that is: *Who is visiting here?*

"So now let's imagine that we're all sweeping. Isn't it something about having the broom in hand, the touch of the actual handle—is it made of wood, for example, or aluminum?—as it moves across the floor slowly, in rhythmic, repetitive motions, and the rasping sound that this makes? Can you hear it?

"Then, it's as if the world opens and quite suddenly it's as though we're being swept into the Imaginal Realm with all the Wise Old Ones of the World, those ever-sweeping, ever-dreaming elders who tend the floors of the mythological world.

"In other words, if we allow ourselves to creatively interweave with the elements and actions that we're aspects of—that indeed we create, so in this case, while sweeping, sweeping can then sweep through our very being, reshaping the place that our sweeping, dreaming, mythological bodies now have in the imaginal sweeping world.

"This is what's called having a 'mythic imagination.' And what it requires from us is an ongoing orientation—a storied and embodied and deeply reverent approach to the things that we generally find most ordinary, to those same things that we might otherwise approach in flat and fixed, decidedly un-storied ways. Oh, if only we could begin to see that this, too, is a story we're telling ourselves about the way things are.

"Change the story!" I say then. "Sweep the old approaches into the dustpan along with the dirt we're sweeping up from the floor, and toss the lot of it into the trash bin!

"For, as Henry Corbin reminds us, there is an element of decision required in spiritual awakening. In other words, we are faced with a choice. Do we want to develop the capacity to see into 'things' as 'beings' or not? The decision to orient oneself toward the search for the hidden-from-plain-view aspect of being, of course, does not guarantee that we'll see anything beyond what's materially present. But we're certainly not going to find the capacity to see what's really there if we're not looking for it, if we decide once and for all that there is nothing else *to* see, or if we simply don't want to see anything else, that is, if we lack both the desire and the wherewithal to practice this way of 'seeing' as an orientation to being. For having a mythic imagination requires not only that we be true to ourselves and to those we love, it also requires the desire to make something of our lives and the work we do, and this takes commitment, the courage of love, and a willingness to practice our lives."

"So the tasks themselves become our great teachers, our yogis and yoginis," the dreamer offers.

"And we their dedicated students," I nod. "And maybe then we might not be in quite so much of a rush to get through the things on our 'to do' lists."

"So it's how we're doing what we're already doing," she repeats.

"Stick with anything long enough, and, mindfully practiced, that is, with the intelligence of the heart—which is a kind of knowing and loving by means of imagining—and it becomes the way," I nod. "This is what is meant by 'radical receptivity.' So let yourself be silently drawn by the stronger pull of what you really love, as Rumi suggests, and what you'll discover is that what you love teaches you how to love. In other words, we learn how to love through what we love, especially when we offer what we love to the world for its sake and for the sake of the Angel of our Being, rather than hoarding it merely for our own personal ends. For what we love when we offer it to the world this way invariably takes us where we would not otherwise go, that is, if it were just left to us."

"Like Ganesha's mount," the fellow across the room offers, "who is the tiniest of tiny, little shrews by the name of Mushika. And Mushika carries Ganesha to all sorts of places that the Elephant God would not have access to without him. And the thing that is so marvelous about the image of this great, pot-bellied Elephant God riding this teeny tiny little mouse," he continues, "is that what would otherwise not be together, that is, in the waking-world of things—because elephants are traditionally terrified of mice—is mythologically brought into working harmony in the same image!"

"So it's rather like the pelicavens moving the monkeys," someone offers.

"Which again reminds us that whenever fear and curiosity are present, curiosity wins. Though fear is much, much bigger in size—a great big elephant of fear, we need only a teeny tiny mouse of curiosity to be able to go all sorts of places that otherwise we would not be able to go.

So we go with fear, that is, with great big fear riding on the back of a little curiosity." Oh, what a truly marvelous image!

"This is the navigational aspect of the heart," I remind them, "along with the educated feeling life that is the focus of so much of our work here. For it's not enough to merely 'feel' these things—the feeling place is only ever the starting point, the 'YOU ARE HERE' with a little red arrow pointing to the precise place on the imaginal map of things. In other words, feelings only indicate to us where the work is, where we ought to pick up the thread of being and begin our weaving. But," I shake my head, "once pinpointed," I raise my arms in the air to make a big elephant head again, "we're instead in the rather disappointing cultural habit of talking 'about' the elephant in order to 'think' it away, in order to exorcise it or mollify the experience with the so-called talking cure, as if this is somehow the work," I shake my head. "It is not.

"Ganesh and Mushika travel together. So it's the kind of thinking that's possible with that great big elephant of emotions, through them, through what we're actually experiencing, because, as Robert Sardello reminds us, 'emotion is the life force of the soul.' So if we can allow the life force of soul to be present, what we find is that we are actually being led to a whole new way of being, where thinking and feeling are experienced as they're occurring, that is, traveling together, through our bodies in the context of the world.

"Feeling, however, is something that few of us are able to do. The poets, of course, 'feel' because poetry is a kind of personification of feeling. The poet e.e. cummings puts it like this:

A poet is somebody who feels, and who expresses his feelings through words.

This may sound easy. It isn't.

A lot of people think or believe or know they feel—but that's thinking or believing or knowing; not feeling. And poetry is feeling—not knowing or believing or thinking.

Almost anybody can learn to think or believe or know, but not a single human being can be taught to feel. Why? Because whenever you think or believe you know, you're a lot of other people: but the moment you feel, you're nobody-but-yourself.

To be nobody-but-yourself—in a world which is doing its best, night and day, to make you everybody else—means to fight the hardest battle which any human being can fight; and never stop fighting.[13]

"But now we have to be careful here, Feelers," I caution. "For if thinking and believing and knowing get muddled up with feeling, the relationship between feeling and emotion is even more fraught. Emotions, as we have said, are the life force of the soul. But they are also wild and uncontrollable, like Nature herself. And, though they are not ours and they do not belong to us, they course through us. If we're not careful then, they can destroy us, and those around us, that is, if we let them.

"Sometimes the destruction of rampant emotions is literal, but all too often it is more subtle, taking the form of a stopped spiritual birth. Thus, one of the goals of working this way is the transformation of these impersonal forces of nature.

"The natural soul must be moved. For it's not enough to just accept what's been given to us; we must make something of it. Soul, like all imaginal practices, needs tending."

"So the whole thing is an opportunity to practice yoga," the dreamer says then, "if we . . . if *I* open up the practices and stop taking them so literally. Then just maybe it might move that monkey."

"Isn't this the hidden gift of the addictions?" someone says then. "Aren't they the dissatisfied soul reminding us of our longing, our humanness?"

"James Hillman says 'we must begin where we are fallen—flat on our backs in personal pain.' But it's important to stress, however, that where we are fallen is only ever the 'starting place.' In other words, 'flat on our backs' is not meant to become a 'permanent abode.' So it helps to orient ourselves to the kind of 'homeing' we were talking about earlier, and to the precise 'call' of our personal pain. Is there a way, in other words, that we, or that you, might suffer for the Angel?"

The dreamer slowly nods. "Suffer *for* the Angel," she softly repeats. And we are visited then by the kind of silence that accompanies the natural endings of things. "Namaste," she says quietly, placing her hands palms together in front of her heart and bowing slightly. "And I want to say that I'm sorry," she adds then. "I didn't mean to take the room hostage."

"It's those pesky monkeys asking to be in the room through you, so there's no apology necessary. We can all find our place in this dream," I add, as several dreamers bobble-head their solidarity. "But now," I continue, as though untying the imaginal thread of Happy Head from around my ring finger, "where were we?"

—————

"You were outing Happy Head in order to highlight that dreams are initiatory," someone offers. "And I asked, 'Why Jesus?'"

"Ah, yes."

"Was the abrupt left turn we just took with the monkey dream a defense against this idea that dreams are callings?" someone asks then.

I shrug. "All that matters is that we bow before what's actually here and bow again before for what's trying to come through from the future that is now. So we endeavor to make enough room for everything, whether it's a lit-from-within-and-trying-to-be-encountered-in-the-world dream image, or a dim and distantly nagging resistance that we experience by going off in one direction instead of another."

Then, "Happy Head," I say, "in answer to your question of 'why Jesus?' It's Happy Head himself who brings me, and now us, into the presence of Jesus. So, though I don't consider myself a Believer, that is, in a 'God created in the faiths,' as Henry Corbin puts it, I'm nonetheless beautifully and deeply and reverently drawn to Jesus, just as I am, for example, to Ganesh. And though I'm not particularly invested in choosing a winner from among the world's three hundred or so existing religions, if, as the Sufis suggest, each of us gets the God we are capable of, well . . . isn't Happy Head the God I am capable of? For what is Happy Head but the divine, the Other, epiphanizing to me in a form that I can love?"

"'The Other epiphanizing to you in a form that you can love,'" someone slowly repeats, trying to let the words penetrate.

"So is it like that thing you wrote after you broke your back?" one of the dreamers asks then.

LECTIO DIVINA OF LOVE

One day not that long ago, while trying to help my daughter and her flyaway pet parrot down from the neighbor's oak, I fell from an extension ladder and landed on a retaining wall. I had to be taken into the emergency room of the local hospital. As they were treating me for a broken back and rib, the trauma physician asked me a host of routine questions about my medical and personal history.

"Do you have a religious preference?"

"No," I answered.

"Any dietary preferences?"

I shook my head as the lab technician started drawing my blood. "But I've been on a bread-and-water fast for the last twenty-eight days," I added, reasoning that the blood tests might come back showing signs of anemia. "I'm trying to make it to thirty."

"Bread-and-water," the physician repeated, tilting his head curiously. "Are you trying to lose weight?" He looked me up and down sideways.

"No," I said. "It's a fast, not a diet."

"Why bread and water?"

"Religious reasons."

"I thought you said you don't have a religious preference?"

"I don't," I said, starting to laugh in spite of myself, then clutching my broken rib. "Oh, Doc, don't make me laugh."

"Ahhhh," he nodded knowingly. "You're hoping to find one."

"Something like that," I smiled.

"You should be Catholic," he leaned in and said then, like a responsible father trying to talk his not-so-pragmatic daughter into buying a more reliable car, while scribbling something into my chart.

"Yes," I said. "But only a little bit."

The next day, when the hospital chaplain came around to visit me in my room, I realized that the doctor had taken our little exchange seriously.

"It says here that you have no religious preference," the chaplain said, looking up from her copy of my admission chart and smiling warmly. I nodded and smiled; it was clear to me that this woman had answered a vocation. "Well," she said. "We just wanted you to know that we're here for you if you need us."

"Thank you," I said.

Then, glancing over at the patient in the next bed, the chaplain looked suddenly quite grim. "It's not easy to live without religion these

days," she added. As if on cue, my eighty-six-year-old roommate,
Josephine, moaned pitifully on the other side of the curtain that divided
our room in half.

"I'll say," I nodded. "But then it's not that I'm trying to live without
religion so much as I am trying to be in friendship with all three hundred
of them," I said to the chaplain. She chuckled and shifted her weight
slightly. Then, after reminding me again that she was there if I needed her
and peering over at poor old Josephine, she left the room.

In the echoing, not-so-silent silence that followed the chaplain's
departure, I began wondering how long I'd be confined to this bed with
Josephine moaning through her oxygen mask on the other side of the
curtain. I started wishing that I could paint again like I did as a child.
I pictured myself Frida Kahlo-like, complete with a soul-patch and
a crown of bright flowers in my hair, painting miniature icons of my
post-modern religious longing. As I imagined painting a blue-breasted,
four-armed female Jesus nailed to the eastern double cross of a telephone
pole, I thought of Sri Ramakrishna, the great Hindu sage who said,
"There can be as many spiritual paths as there are spiritual aspirants, and
as many gods as there are devotees." A sign I once saw on the walls of a
monastery read:

> The God you are seeking
> is also seeking you. The desire you sense
> is God's invitation and gift. You have a choice.
> How will you respond?

What would such a God look like, I wonder? I'm expecting the
slow, six-centuries-long, deep-breathing birth of a God fused from the
gods and goddesses of the world's three hundred religions, burning with
desire for the canvas through the bristles of the sable brush in my hand. A
God longing for new shapes, colors, and sizes, and seeking to deepen the

mysteries of the heart. Love is the only religion I'll give my life to again and again; a perpetually professed sister practicing the *lectio divina* of Love. Everything else is just squabbling over details.

⁓

"This is as a response to breaking my back, written while recovering and confined to my bed," I answer then. "And it's directly related to the dream of Happy Head though there are . . . what?—some fifteen or so waking-world years between them, that is, between Happy Head making himself known to me in a dream, and then me breaking my back. Though just saying it like this tends to put events into a 'chronological order'— another thing that the dreamtime is rather unconcerned with, except in a 'when/then' unfolding sort of way."

"I'm curious," one of the dreamers asks. "Why were you on a bread-and-water fast? It seems so 'prison.'"

"I was fasting for—get this—*clarity*."

"Oooooh, be careful what you wish for."

"Right?" I chuckle. "How the longing for clarity might be answered by the soul/spirit realms was simply beyond my imaginative capacities at the time. It was immediately and abundantly clear, however, that I broke my back in two places, that I broke a rib, and that I punctured my spleen."

"What about the kind of clarity you were fasting for?"

"The word 'clarity' means 'transparency to itself,' and it refers to a kind of thinking that bears its own inner significance. In other words, it doesn't need to refer to anything else in order to be comprehended. But I didn't really know that then," I say. "I was merely asking for help with understanding what I was going through."

"Because?"

"Because I'd fallen hopelessly in love. And I just couldn't fathom why? Or why it was such an utterly impossible love, with no chance whatsoever of blossoming into anything tangible and concrete in the waking-world of things. And why no matter how hard I tried, and regardless of what I tried—and believe me, I tried everything!—the in-love-ness just wouldn't leave me alone?

"So after many years of torment, and with several rather blunt, very embarrassing, and indeed very clear indications that it was never going to amount to anything other than an affair of the heart, I began to get curious about what the love could possibly want from me besides an actual relationship with the object, that is, the person, of my desire. What did the madness of being in love want? And so that's why I was fasting. To get help with this."

"*And?*"

"The mystery continues," I smile, "even as it deepens."

"Awww," a few in the room moan with disappointment.

"That said," I smile, "there are several transparent tributaries that now lead from the experience. The in-love-ness, for example, that is, with an actual waking-world person, has mercifully folded up its tent and moved on, looking for some other unsuspecting soul to rattle and bodily possess, no doubt. But now the whole thing," I make a large circle in the air, "Happy Head and falling into impossible love and breaking my back, seems entirely related to the kind of 'divine madness' that Plato talks about in the *Phaedrus*.

"To Plato, you may recall, Socrates possessed a divine wisdom. Led by divine inspiration and a genuine passion for philosophy, and the appropriate realities of its quest, Plato imagined that if Socrates was indeed a fool, as those around him were suggesting, then he was god's fool, for his, according to Plato, was a sublime lunacy. Therefore, Plato concludes that when madness is a gift from the gods it is superior to 'sanity,' for it is the source of our greatest happiness.

"Though there are several kinds of divine madness imagined by the ancient Greeks, Plato cites four examples:

1. From Apollo, the gift of prophesy
2. From Dionysus, the mystic rites and relief from present hardship
3. From the Muses, poetry
4. From Aphrodite, love

The madness of love, therefore, is a gift bestowed upon us by Aphrodite.

"While recovering from my broken back," I lean back and look up to the ceiling. "I was confined to bed. For weeks on end the only direction I could look was up. But now it might be easy to miss the significance of this, if you didn't also know that I'd spent years—decades, in fact— looking only down and around and just so, in the direction of dreams, of soul and the underworld, due to a natural affinity with the soul direction of things, with basements and the dark."

"Because of that time with your sister?"

"Well, it's the other way around. It's not *because* of that time with my sister. Remember we come in with stories, with natural soul conditions looking to get worked with and through. So it's more that I came into the world with an affinity for basements, and the dark, and the downward direction of soul. But this wasn't revealed to me until that particular incident with my sister down in our basement."

"So when you 'let yourself be silently drawn by the stronger pull of what you really love,' down and around in dreams and toward the image of Happy Head, is that towards your destiny?" someone asks.

"The word 'destiny' originally meant to be 'in life.' So yes, it is Happy Head who remembers me forward. Yet the pull toward life is not meant to be for me, or at least not me alone, so it's not meant to be taken personally. The pull toward life, which takes us invariably deeper and deeper into the mysteries of the heart, is meant to be for the sake of life itself, for the sake of the world. So we want to ask: *What does the pull want?*"

"And yet without you Happy Head would not even be."

"Precisely. For Happy Head does not exist except through me. So what this reveals is actually rather startling, for it suggests that the body I call 'mine' is not mine at all, or at least, not only mine. And this," I pause, "is the 'clarity' I was granted from the soul/spirit realms when I broke my back.

"When the doctor came into the triage unit that day and relayed the extent of my injuries, my very first thought was: 'Well, at least I know now that I'm not my back.' And then I thought: 'What a bizarre thing to think!' This naturally led to the next philosophical consideration: 'Well, where precisely is the line? In other words, just how much of this body I call "mine" could be taken away before the "I" that's being referred to whenever I say "I" would cease to be?'

"Up until this point in my life, this body I call mine was just something I carted around, rather like a suitcase that I'd bust out whenever the need arose. I never once considered this body as a living, sacred entity entrusted to my care. Nor did I have any inkling that I share this body with the Angel of my Being.

"But this is the difference between image as idol and image as icon," I suggest. "With Happy Head as 'idol,' I tried everything I could think of to make a Happy Head relationship 'happen' in the concrete world of things, that is, with a substantial, embodied lover. As 'icon,' on the other hand, Happy Head allows me to see through him, with him, and specifically *through* the waking-world lover, to what capacities of soul I'm being asked to uniquely develop for his sake, that is, for Happy Head's sake. The all-loving, all-comforting, divine embrace of Happy Head is what calls me deeper and deeper into soul, into spirit, and into bodily life precisely, because as Henry Corbin reminds us, 'it's not our individuation that matters but the individuation of the Angel that is our task.'"

"So are you saying that you share your body with . . ." one of the dreamers hesitates, "Happy Head?"

"Yes, but not only Happy Head. Remember, the language of dreams is not literal, so this is true of *all* dream images. They cannot exist without us. Simply put, they have nowhere else to be; they can only be in this world, this concrete world," I tap my knees, "through us, through our dreaming bodies. It was Happy Head, however, who revealed this to me."

"Are you suggesting then that the dream image of Happy Head knew that you would give up everything to go off in search of him? And that's why he came to you the way he did in the first place?" someone asks, sounding more than a little skeptical. "Because he knew that you would go off in search of him?"

"And that you would fall into an impossible love?" the person next to her chimes in.

"And that the excruciating impossibility of it would eventually cause me to look up to the spiritual worlds?" Then, "Yes," I answer. "This is what I mean when I say that we're being 'remembered forward by the dreamtime.'"

"Doesn't that seem . . ." she smiles and trails off.

"Far-fetched?" I offer. "Absolutely, and yet no more far-fetched than God talking to Moses in a burning bush. It's not meant to be taken literally." Then, "If we look back over any dream that has penetrated us, that has found its true mark, we will see all of the many and varied roads that lead away from it, and that eventually lead back to it. The imaginal possibilities of dreams continue to unfold before us even as we unfold out into the world. James Hillman reminds us this is the way that dreams love us. In other words, if we can move out of an archival stance, we can begin to see, really see, that dreams are happening now and now and now, in an ever-unfolding way, just as we are.

"So dream images are rather like ritual in this way. The ceremonial aspects of ritual are merely the 'illuminated' parts, the 'lit up' bits. The images as we originally receive them in dreams are likewise merely the illuminated aspects, yet if we consent to a kind of companioning of them, if we allow ourselves to enter into loving friendship with them, they continue to 'light the way.'

"Now," I go on, "if Moses had taken others—friends and skeptics alike—with him to that pasture where the Burning Bush spoke to him, would they have seen what he saw, heard what he heard?"

"If a tree falls in the forest . . ."

"The voice of God in the Burning Bush is experienced uniquely *through* Moses," I say. Then, trying to come at it another way, "No one else heard Jack say, 'Make me, make me, make me. I want to be part of your family.' His voice was heard only through me, through my ears. Does that make what I heard so clearly, so distinctly, so repeatedly not real? Unreal? His insistent and incessant calling to me from the other side is not something that can be experienced objectively, or collectively, in the substantial realm of things."

"So what's the difference between hearing Jack's voice, for example, like you did, and hearing voices as crazy people do?"

"Not a whole heck of a lot," I laugh. "Except perhaps the robustness of the individual's ego structure. People who hear voices the whole time have often stopped hearing their own altogether. In other words, they have lost a sense of themselves as individuals and are only hearing voices, or at least hearing voices a good deal of the time.

"But what I'm wondering now," I say, turning to the vocal skeptic in the room, "is if Jack's being here, through the narrowest of circumstances, the smallest of gates, is evidence enough for you that I did not make him up? Or that I did not merely make him up?"

"Couldn't it just be luck?" she offers. "And the science of what happens when two people come together in the dark?"

"It could. But which is a better story? That is, a more creative, imaginative story, one that expands the possibilities of our being and becoming? Because here again we want to invoke that aspirating power of the heart which suggests that through acts of meditating, conceiving, imagining, and ardently desiring, the heart's ability to think is developed and expanded to the point that it makes real a being *external to the person*.

"*Himma* is a form of prayer," I continue. "It's not a prayer that is a request for something—rather it is 'a means of existing and of *causing to exist*.' It is, therefore, 'the supreme act of the Creative Imagination,' according to Henry Corbin.

"So the voice of Jack was both his longing to be in the world through me, as a substantial being, an image become visible, a form 'aspiring to issue forth from his unknowness' through me, and, from the moment I first heard his voice, my desire to make his form known. Or perhaps before even before that, though I was unaware of my longing."

"So then you imagined him into being?"

"Yes, but it was not only me. In other words, I wasn't even aware that there was a Jack-Being trying to be in the fleshly world of things until I heard his voice calling to me from the other side. Was I unconsciously creating his voice? Perhaps." I shrug. "But it certainly wasn't experienced like that. I heard his voice specifically—loud and clear and very insistent. It never wavered or deviated: 'Make me, make me, make me. I want to be part of your family.' So I would say that it was the Angel of Jack's Being—his soul twin, or *daimon*, as the ancient Greeks call it—longing to become actualized through Jack, to have a substantial body and being, which, in turn, was trying to happen through me, by giving birth to Jack."

"And the same is true of Happy Head?"

"Well, I'm not trying to give birth to him the same way I did with Jack," I chuckle, "but yes. Certainly there is a resonance, a 'sympathy of being,' in the way that we as mothers share our bodies with another for their sake, for their eventual being in the world," I pause to consider this. Then, "What are dreams but the descent of the divine and the assumption of the sensible?"

"The descent of the divine and the assumption of the sensible," the woman next to me repeats slowly, reaching for her dream journal.

"The descent of the divine and the assumption of the sensible . . . by way of the underworld," I add then.

"Has Happy Head appeared in any subsequent dreams?"

"None that I'm able to remember."

"Well, why would he make such a dramatic appearance and then disappear altogether?"

"Why indeed!" Then, "Any guesses?"

"Isn't it because absence creates presence?" someone offers.

"Okay," I say. "But now let's play with this idea of who is absent. In the Koran, you may recall, God doesn't say, 'I am *sometimes* closer to you than your own jugular vein.' And in the Gospels Jesus doesn't say, 'The kingdom of God is *sometimes* within you.' So there is no such thing, really, as the absence of the Other; it is only ever our absence from 'Who' is present."

"Isn't his disappearance from dreams because you are being asked to become Happy Head?" someone offers then. "Because if he came in subsequent dreams it might be easy to fall into the trap of believing that he's 'only' an image, or only available to you 'over there' in dreams, that is, as a nighttime only dream figure?"

"Ah, very good . . . so perhaps our Happy Heads disappear from dreaming view to help us understand that these divine images are not

'over there' outside of us, nor are the 'over there' in the archived pages
of our dream journals, they are within our very being. Indeed, they
are us. Yet so excessive is this nearness, according to the Sufis, that at
first it acts as a veil. Which is why the inexperienced novice," I point to
myself, "goes looking for it outside, into the concrete world of things, in
a desperate search from form to form. In his poem 'Too Beautiful,' Hafiz
puts it like this:

The fire
Has roared near you.
The most intimate parts of your body
Got scorched,

So
Of course you have run
From your marriages into a
Different
House

That will shelter you
From embracing every aspect of Him.

God has
Roared near us.
The lashes on our heart's eye got burnt.
Of course we have
Run away

From His
Sweet flaming breath
That proposed an annihilation
Too real,

Too
Beautiful.[14]

"Until, with a bit of luck, a bit of grace, we are at long last returned to the sanctuary of our souls, where we finally begin to perceive that the real Beloved is deep within. And from that moment on, we seek the Beloved only through the Beloved. For the divine Lover, as Henry Corbin reminds us, is spirit without body. The purely physical lover, on the other hand, is body without spirit. But now the spiritual lover, that is, the mystic lover, has both body and spirit. This 'body' that the mystic lover has, however, is ours, so we're con-spiring with one another. We share the breath of being in the same body."

"So how we breathe matters," someone offers.

"Well, that's certainly what William Stafford says, in 'Being a Person':

> Be a person here.
> Stand by the river, invoke the owls.
> Invoke winter, then spring.
> Let any season that wants to come here make its own call.
> After that sound goes away, wait.
> A slow bubble rises through the earth
> and begins to include sky, stars, all space,
> even the outracing, expanding thought.
> Come back and hear the little sound again.
> [Come back, and hear that call.]
> Suddenly this dream you are having matches
> everyone's dream, and the result is the world.
> If a different call came there wouldn't be any
> world, or you, or the river, or the owls calling.
> How you stand here is important.
> How you listen for the next things to happen.
> How you breathe.[15]"

"So . . . is this the 'spirit of Truth whom the world cannot receive' from the Gospel of John?" someone asks. "'For it does not see Him nor know Him, but you will know Him, for He is ever with you and will be in you.'"

"Like Happy Head!" the woman next to me suddenly exclaims.

"Like *all* dreams," I say. "Only not as in something we do. But rather in terms of *yaro yaro*—everything dreaming all the time."

"So we're being asked to develop the capacities of soul that would allow us to see through our dreams to the dream of life?"

"To the dream that is ever-dreaming us and the world into being," I nod.

"Therefore we don't want to confuse historical Jesus with experiencing the kind of love and longing that initiates us into experiencing dreams as the conspiring Presence in an ongoing way?" someone asks.

"Well, isn't the historical problem one of resurrection?" I ask then. "Doesn't it have everything to do with establishing a living 'umbilical' connection between inner and outer events, between the microcosm and the macrocosm? So in what way does the world, which presents itself as 'outside' us, live *in* us, so that we are at once the world and the world is us, so that how we listen, how we breathe, matters? We are each of us given living, dreaming presences that, like Happy Head, are called to intercede on our behalf. And even though each of us will have to come at the dream of what it means to be human in his or her own unique way, if we're at all to develop this capacity for seeing into what's really there, it will necessarily include, indeed require, allowing both love and the imagination to be present."

"In the Gospel of Mary Magdalene," the woman next to me says, "there's a marvelous passage where Mary enters a visionary state and 'sees' Jesus in the realm of the underworld. And so she asks him then whether this state of seeing is one of soul or of spirit. To which Jesus replies, 'It is neither the soul nor the spirit, it is the heart.' Of course," she continues, "if we've ever really experienced love we already know that it's a mode of 'seeing.'"

"And isn't this what we're being initiated into? Isn't this way of seeing, with both love and the imagination present, actually what's trying to be initiated into the world through Jesus and Mary Magdalene?"

The kind of initiation that love and the imagination offers is readily available to one and all through the images that are present in dreams if we are willing to live with these lit-from-within images in an ongoing way, across decades of time, and perhaps even lifetimes, turning them over and ever over, concentrating on them, and with them, and for them, entering the temple of being, and trying to get a feel for the light that shines through them, befriending them and introducing them to ever-fresh, ever-greening occurrences of inner life and outer observations, even as we unfold with them out into the world.

"Your dream experience strikes me as quite similar to many near-death experiences I've read about," one of the dreamers offers then. "The hallmark of which is an overwhelming longing to go toward the light and keep going. Which strikes me as going away from this earthly, bodily life toward the spirit realms."

"Well, certainly during the dream 'I' feel the pull towards unity with Happy Head and not the agony of being a body-in-time, because, of course, the being-in-time's body is asleep, right? Renée Dreaming is in her bed. But in Happy Head's arms and relieved of all fear, 'I' am all but dissolved in his embrace. Until the dream of 'being with him' itself begins to dissolve. And then 'I' feel myself acutely, that is, Renée Dreaming and dreaming 'I' are experienced in dynamic tension, bodily and imaginally, between, on the one side, the pull towards life, towards the waking-world of physical, in-time being; and on the other hand, Happy Head and his most beautiful, eternal, and bodily-dissolving embrace.

"And it's the dawning realization during the dream that I am dreaming—and that I will eventually waken—that causes me to suffer so exquisitely," I continue. "There is something so familiar in Happy Head's embrace, and it is something that I recognize. And in that remembered and familiar, holy and human embrace, I don't ever want to leave. But it's this that awakens me precisely in an ongoing way to my longing. The answer to our longing, as Rumi reminds us in his poem 'Love Dogs,' however, is more longing."

One Night a man was crying *Allah! Allah!*
His lips grew sweet with praising,
until a cynic said, "So!
I have heard you calling out, but have you ever
gotten any response?"

The man had no answer to that.
He quit praying and fell into a confused sleep.

He dreamed he saw Khidr, the guide of souls,
in a thick, green foliage.

"Why did you stop praising?" "Because
I've never heard anything back."

"This longing you express
is the return message."

The grief you cry out from
draws you toward union.

Your pure sadness
that wants help
is the secret cup.

Listen to the moan of a dog for its master.
That whining is the connection.

There are love dogs
no one knows the names of.

Give your life
to be one of them.[16]

"Isn't Khdir a greening-into-being-guide-to-souls that—like the
ever-green patch on the Mount Hood iceberg—reminds us again and
again of our ever-greening possibilities for a return to the garden within,
to home, and the ongoing home we're lending ourselves to in order to
become co-creators of Earth?"

Then, "But somehow I understand, in that heavy, heavy halfway
place between sleeping and waking, that if I ever want to get back into
Happy Head's eternal embrace, it has to be through this life, through this
physical, in-time-being's body," I pat my thighs for dramatic emphasis,
"and all that the soul saw while standing on the other side, during the
dream, and long before it even. All that's required, really, is that we live
the lives our souls agreed to live before being born into the crushing
world of time."

"So what's that?" someone asks. "I mean, specifically, for you?"

"That," I smile, "is the sort of thing that takes an entire lifetime to
discover. That is, if we're lucky. There are strange pop-up clues along the
way, however, that seem to ask for our attention specifically."

A BEAUTY WORTH FIGHTING FOR

Once, when I was about eleven years old, a couple of girlfriends were
over. We were on our way upstairs to my bedroom to play some sort of
dating game with imaginary boyfriends when one of the girls stopped
next to the console television set, which was angled in the corner of the
living room. "Ewww!" she cupped one hand over her mouth and with the
other hand pointed at the only piece of "art" in our home.

It was one of those bonded Carrara copies that were so popular in
the 70s. This one, a sculpture by Giambologna known as "The Rape of

the Sabine Women," depicted three idealized naked figures posed around a spiral axis—a man, taut limbs and muscles bulging, lifts a woman into the air, while a second man crouches dramatically between his legs, looking up. The original piece was intended as nothing more than a demonstration of the artist's ability to create a complex sculptural group from a single block of marble. Later, its subject matter—the mythical rape of the Sabines—had to be invented when the Grand Duke of Tuscany, Francesco de' Medici, put it on public display in the Piazza della Signoria.

"Ewww!" my friend squealed again, turning eyes-wide to gape at the other girl. "Look at his wie-ner!"

The other girl calmly reached around then and goosed the standing man's sculpted butt as both girls burst into peals of hysterical eleven-year-old laughter and fell onto the floor. But instead of falling on the floor along with them, I became incensed, passionately irate.

"Art," I scolded, placing my hands emphatically on my hips, "is not pornographic! It is not anything to be mocked at or . . ."

Well, this made them laugh even more. I became so impassioned then that I kicked them out of our house, telling them that I never wanted to see them again.

Sitting there trembling on my bed after the whole incident, I wondered, "*What on earth was that all about?*" Then it struck me that "art" was something I was willing to fight for. The idea of "art," though I didn't really know much about "art" at all, was something beautiful that I experienced in the deepest, most sincere part of myself, and it was something, evidently, that I was willing to lose friends over.

It occurred to me then that I was odd in an odd way, and likewise peculiar. I was not "adopted" as my older sister liked to tease me; I knew that my family was indeed mine and that we belonged to one another in a blood and bones way. I did not think that I was in the wrong family, nor did I believe that I was born in the wrong place or time. I just understood, quite suddenly, that I was unlike most anyone I had ever met. And I began to see myself within a larger context.

For the first time ever, and though I couldn't even name it then, I understood that I was an artist. I experienced the realm of the beautiful more fully, more artistically than anyone I knew. When I kicked my two friends out of the house for laughing at the nakedness in our "art," what incensed me was their inability to see the hidden-from-plain-view otherness that I experienced as something utterly and undeniably beautiful.

The thing that moved me with that little statue, however, was not so much the statue itself—that is, with what it depicted. Nor was it the considerable skill with which it was rendered by the artist. Rather, it was that there had been someone who had been struck by an artistic intention, however many years before, someone moved so deeply by that intention that "art" resulted. That to me, even at a very young age, was a beauty worth fighting for.

What became even more clear to me that afternoon was that as soon as I was old enough I would have to go off in search of my clan, in search of others who were likewise odd and peculiar. I was certain that such a clan existed because there was beauty in the world and there was art.

Looking back, I can see that finding a clan has less to do with searching for other individuals who might belong to the same clan and more to do with recognizing my particular and individualized style for being in the world.

———

"So having a particular style, we could say, is another one of the threads we come in with. In other words, it's fated. And we're being asked to take responsibility for these fated aspects of being."

"But not to change them?"

"They can't be changed. Fated things are allotted. We're merely being asked to recognize them in order that we might begin to take some responsibility for the various ways that they display themselves."

"So there's no way we can change our fate?"

"Well, perhaps there's a way to trick it," I say. "Like in that old line, 'I didn't have a penny to my name—so I changed my name.' In other words, there are ways to work with fate, alongside it, rather than merely against it, or by throwing in the towel in a fatalistic way.

"I know of a woman, for example, who has several advanced degrees. But now she also has quite a violent temper. On one occasion she got so angry that she threw her daughter into the microwave in their kitchen and gashed her cheek, leaving quite a dramatic scar. Some time later, as she was recounting the event while showing me her daughter's scar, she said, 'Everyone knows that I have a violent temper when I haven't had enough to eat,' she shrugged. 'So they're just going to have to learn how to stick clear of me when I get like that.' But, of course, this is not at all what I'm suggesting either. This is fate as fatalism, which, as evidenced by this example, is no good either.

"So, while there is a kind of bowing before our fated circumstances, those things about us that cannot be changed, like, for example, our height, there are other things, qualities and behavioral tendencies, like violently losing one's temper, that are indeed asking to be grappled with."

"When Jacob wrestles that Angel," someone offers, "we never learn what they're fighting about; we only know that it's a fight almost to the death."

"Some fated things are obvious. While other fated aspects are made known to us only slowly, over time, when we're ready to work with what's revealed. We can't really begin grappling with these less-than-obvious-to-us fated aspects of being that have been allotted to us—whether we believe that we've chosen them or not—until it's revealed just what they are."

"And this is something that the dreamtime is always trying to do? Reveal this to us?"

"Yes," I say, "as we're ready to receive the information. Which is a good thing to remember because it's rather counter-intuitive," I add. "In other words, we get the crushing dreams—the sort that bring death as an immediate kind of seeing-through—when we can, that is, when we are spiritually and psychologically robust enough to handle what's being revealed to us, and what's being asked of us.

"Of course, it doesn't feel like this to the dreamer, for as Carl Jung reminds us, 'every victory for the soul is experienced as a defeat by the ego.' So if we can remind ourselves that dreams are trying to love us into a bigger, more beautiful story that is trying to unfold through us into the world, then these undoing dreams might even be seen, at least on a soul level, as rather encouraging.

"On the other hand, we tend to get the deeply encouraging kinds of dreams when we must. When they are more or less required in order for us to go on, when without them we might fold up the tent of soul altogether, becoming consumers and tourists, or mere hedonists. Or when we're dangerously close to dropping the project of who we're becoming altogether."

"What do you make of that handicapped guy?" someone asks then, circling back to the dream.

"Well, isn't is because I'm a bit 'handicapped' in the old thinking department?" I tap the side of my temple.

"Well, you can hardly be considered 'mentally disabled.'"

"Not literally, of course, but for two reasons. First, because thinking—that is, abstract thinking, disengaged from the feeling life—for us feelers always lags behind. It's just the nature of the set-up—which has everything to do, again, with one's 'style' for being. But if we learn to work with this, that is, feeling our way along in the dark *with* the lagging-behind thinking life, all the while trying to practice patience and compassion—well then, what more can be asked of us?

"On the other hand, we need to constantly undeceive ourselves. For the woman who is not to be trusted and the all brawn, no brains characters are also aspects of 'me,' that is, of the twofold side of being of Renée Dreaming in Mystical Poverty. And these aspects, which display themselves so clearly in the dream, have no compunction whatsoever about using the mentally disabled fellow for their own ends. So again, this is why working in small, dedicated groups is so valuable . . . because there is always a tendency to deceive ourselves by feigning a kind of deliberate obtuseness, or perhaps by merely looking the other way.

"But now, returning to the image, isn't being 'mentally disabled' actually required if we are ever to learn the navigational wisdom that's being offered to us in the thinking/feeling heart realm of the soul?" I ask. "Are we not being asked to refrain from all the secondary thinking 'about' things—which is never anything other than moving what we already know, what's already familiar to us, into clever, intriguing, and seemingly new patterns? Like in those square puzzles that we thumb the little numbered tiles around?"

"'Don't be clever, be intelligent. Any fool can be clever.' That's what my mother used to say," someone offers.

"So long as this intelligence doesn't fool us into believing that we know anything," I add. "So we'll want to continually invoke Socrates, who considered his main task to be care of the soul, though he regularly stated that he really didn't really know anything at all about the soul."

"So the trick is to always proceed from a not-knowing place, letting go of our assumptions and preconceived notions?" someone asks.

"Like 'beginner's mind,'" someone else adds. "The Zen master Shunryu Suzuki says, 'In the beginner's mind there are many possibilities, in the expert's mind there are few.'"

"I'm thinking about the so-called 'observer effect' in physics," someone then says, "where the observation of a thing changes it. That is, in answer to your earlier question about why Happy Head has disappeared from any subsequent dreams."

"Well, okay, but I think we'll want to imagine that it's not a one-way street. In other words, it's not merely 'our' observation of a thing that changes it—though it may appear that way to those without the kind of vision that is capable of seeing that whatever we're looking at is likewise looking back."

"You mean *it's* seeing *us*?"

"And so it's the exchange between us that changes things," I nod, "not just the thing we're observing, but also us; we are changed by being observed, even as we're observing. So the exchange is transfigurational."

"So is this why you said that the mystery of Happy Head continues and deepens?"

"Because it's still unfolding. When I awoke from the dream of Happy Head, just like Joseph in the Biblical story we discussed earlier, I don't think that I really woke up at all. Indeed, all the dream managed to awaken then, almost twenty years ago, was my longing. When I left the life I was living to go off in search of Happy Head, when I fell into an impossible love, and later even, when I broke my back, just like Joseph, I was still sleeping. And, if we're to accept the Koran's version of things, I still am!" I shrug. "And maybe, as the Koran suggests, we all are, and this is precisely what it means to be human.

"But it was only by finally looking up while confined to that hospital bed, with old Josephine moaning on the other side of that curtain, that I began to experience the Beloved within. It was only then that I began to fall in love—madly and deeply and devotedly—with the longing itself. It was only then that I started to become one of the love dogs that Rumi writes about.

"But, as the dream is still unfolding, I'm still endeavoring to 'give my life' to be a love dog. In other words, we don't find the Happy Heads, or the Jesuses, or the Mount Hood Icebergs or the Whimpering Creatures of the world once and for all—for not only are they an ongoing orientation to being, they are ever unfolding, just as we are, just as the world continues to be created in an ongoing way.

"But what we do discover, finally, is that the very things we're after are also after us—if only we could get inwardly still and openly receptive enough to let their presence be revealed to us. The dreamtime invites us to accept the task of becoming who we are really, but who we are is not for ourselves alone. It's for the sake of the images and the dream of the world. For these images and the dream of the world cannot be known, even unto themselves, that is, if ever, except through us."

"Joseph Campbell said that the 'privilege of a lifetime is becoming who you are,'" someone offers.

"Well, dreams are here to remind us that it's damn hard work! Because who we are is not given, except in potential. And even though we're all born with precisely the right medicine to become ourselves, we must endeavor to go out into the world to have this revealed to us, in order that we might get access to the medicine we're carrying."

"So it's not by chance that you have to run through a World Cup soccer final in order to get to Happy Head." the woman next to me says, looping back to the dream. "This is life and death stuff!"

"Which brings us round to 'divine madness,'" I say. "And the Myth of the Charioteer."

MYTH OF THE CHARIOTEER

In the last third of the *Phaedrus*, Plato introduces us to a Charioteer who has a team of two horses. Unlike the gods, however, who have two good horses, the Charioteer has one good horse and one, well . . . not so good horse. Now, the good horse—considered a "friend of honor"—is a noble steed and is pliant therefore to the commands of the Charioteer. The not-so-noble steed, on the other hand, is unruly and intractable, viciously fractious, disobedient to the rule of the Charioteer, and outrageously bent upon sensuous satisfactions.

But now there is another general characteristic of soul introduced in this myth. Plato tells us that individual souls are winged. And it's with these wings that chariot-riding souls endeavor to lift themselves up to where the gods dwell. Yet even the most dedicated souls are barely able to raise their chariots up to the rim of the arena, where they can look out upon what Plato calls "reality," because, like the Charioteer, they have to deal with their two horses.

So these winged, chariot-riding souls rise and fall at varying times, seeing some things and, of course, missing others. When lifted-up souls get even the smallest glimpse of the truth of their being, that is, when they are nourished and grow in the presence of wisdom and goodness and the beauty of the divine, their soul-wings grow, which, in turn, naturally increases their lifting powers.

Eventually, however, because of the difficulty with their horses, or having fallen into forgetfulness, souls lose their wings and fall back down to Earth, where they are incarnated into different kinds of persons. Those souls that have been initiated—because of what they have seen and can remember from up there in the arena of the gods—become "philosophers" and "lovers of beauty" who are "dedicated to love."

And this, Plato tells us, is the divine madness bestowed upon us by love here on Earth. In other words, seeing beauty, the soul is reminded of the true beauty it glimpsed when, lifted up, it saw beyond heaven to what Plato calls "reality." For Beauty, we are told, is among the most radiant things to see beyond heaven. And here on Earth it sparkles through vision, the clearest of our senses. Love on Earth, then, according to Plato, is but a reflection of the love of what the soul saw.

So it follows that, upon catching sight of a beautiful lover, we are startled and overcome with the memory of what the soul saw. However, it's at this point that some souls mistake this reminder of beauty and instead pursue the pleasures. But this is not "divine madness" at all, says Plato, for it merely indicates that one has lost one's head.

They are other souls that, according to the story, though equally startled and overcome with the memory of beauty upon seeing the beautiful lover, who experience only the utmost joy. The wings of these souls begin to grow even more. When separated from the beautiful lover, however, these same souls experience such intense pain and longing that their wings begin to harden. Caught between joy, on the one hand, and intense pain and longing on the other, the lover of Beauty experiences anguish.

But now when the Charioteer gazes into the eyes of the beautiful one he loves, his noble horse is controlled by its sense of shame, while his not-so-noble horse, completely overcome with desire, does everything it can think of to seduce the beautiful lover. Eventually, the not-so-noble horse wears the Charioteer and the noble horse down, dragging them toward the beautiful lover with promises of pleasurable sex.

When the Charioteer looks again upon the face of the beautiful lover, however, he is carried immediately back to the "reality" he experienced while navigating his chariot in the arena of the gods. He pulls violently on the reins over and over again, until at last, the not-so-noble horse is brought under the Charioteer's command, whereupon the Charioteer is allowed to pursue his lover in reverence and in awe, and the lover is allowed to reciprocate.

If the lovers manage to somehow get through this desire, their souls are returned to heaven, for they will have displayed a perfect combination of human self-control and divine madness. Those who give in to their desires, will nonetheless have to keep trying until they get it right, until they too grow wings, and, weightless once again, are returned to heaven.

———

"So now what strikes you, if anything, upon hearing this myth on the heels of the Happy Head dream?"

"Well, I'm quite struck by the fact that Happy Head's embrace seems to be a recollection of what the soul saw, lifted up there in the arena of the gods," someone offers.

"To what Plato calls 'reality,'" I nod. "Anything else?"

"The two horses," the woman next to me says. "The not-so-noble steed strikes me as the dream horse that's chasing you, with the woman who is not to be trusted on its back."

"Breathing and foaming all over me," I lift my hand to evoke the horse over my shoulder, "and driving me into the arms of Happy Head."

"Isn't this because, in a sense, we need to be tricked or forced or compelled into going where we would not venture if things were just left to us, that is, to the familiar part of us?" someone suggests. "If things were just left to the ego?"

"Oh, yes! I'd still be back in the kitchen of that barn-shaped house chatting with the handicapped guy!" I chuckle.

"At the beginning of the Book of John, Jesus says to Peter, 'Very truly, I tell you, when you were younger, you used to fasten your own belt and go wherever you wished. But when you grow old, you will stretch out your hands, and someone else will fasten a belt around you and take you where you do not wish to go.'

"Well, what is the belt that gets fastened around us if not the belt of dreams?" I ask then. "The dreamtime belt takes us where we do not wish to go, that is, where we do not wish to go as narrow ego-beings."

"The noble steed," the woman beside me adds, "strikes me as the Horse of Dreams, the imaginal one that we are invited to ride out on when hearing into a dream."

"When I hear this myth," I nod, "I'm struck by just how much it bears a rather uncanny resemblance to the whole initiation. And though there are simply too many details to go into, we can notice the highlights. We can notice, therefore, Happy Head's original appearance and his remembered embrace, falling into an impossible love and trying everything possible to seduce the beautiful lover, which eventually led to the opening insights that managed to find their way to me, through my broken back."

"I'm struck by why the noble steed is 'controlled by its sense of shame' when it looks upon the face of the beautiful lover?" someone asks.

"For Plato," I say, "the soul is 'prophetic' in that it has an irrepressible love of Being that impels the 'lover of wisdom' ever onward in the pursuit of truth. In other words, we are being loved forward, remembered into being by what the soul saw—while standing on the other side in the *Myth of Er*, or up and around in the arena of gods in this myth—when, riding those chariots, we looked out and saw 'reality.' Therefore, as lovers of wisdom, Plato says that we are required to always make the best choices 'with an eye on soul,' in other words, with certain consideration for what the soul saw.

"Now it's important to remember, however, that the ancient Greeks were not separate from nature as we are, so they were still experiencing thought and being together. In other words, our history has not yet happened, so the divorce between thought and being has not yet taken place. Thus, when Plato instructs us to make the best choice with an eye on soul, the lover of wisdom is not being instructed to think 'about' things, as we moderns are apt to do, and then make the best choice. No,

Plato is telling the lover of wisdom to think *into* the best choice, feeling our way along in the dark based on what the soul saw and can remember.

"Shame, then, according to Plato, is the telltale sign of contrariety in the human spirit. Its presence lets us know that we have made a less than best choice where matters of the soul are concerned. Its presence therefore lets us in on the simple truth that, indeed, we do know better. So shame, as the inward monitor that chides, is but a thinly disguised manifestation of the higher love that the lover of wisdom is slowly remembering and endeavoring to pursue.

"Though every bit as taken with the beautiful lover as the not-so-noble steed, the noble steed is guided by his ability to make the best choice with an eye on soul—*through desire*. And it's this that keeps him from acting on purely libidinous impulses, at least until the not-so-noble steed wears him and the Charioteer down."

"This is a whole different way of understanding shame," someone says. "It's shame as encounter, based on what the soul saw."

"What the soul saw and can remember," someone adds.

"Isn't this is why the Old Ones say that behind shame is radiance? Because we are being remembered into being who we are really?"

"Through desire?"

"Through desire, yes, just as in Dante's *Divine Comedy*. So it's important that we don't take 'desire' too literally here to mean merely sexual desire. Sexual desire is but one of the desires; one that is, imaginally speaking, generally easy to engage. But Plato, like our friend Dante, says that all desire leads to God—because souls are winged and aimed—and that love of anything is a remembrance of the love of what the soul saw."

"So souls have no chance of growing wings by merely getting above desire, or by trying to get beyond it, or repressing it or whatever?"

"The soul grows its wings through desire, through the presence of desire and by learning to bring the not-so-noble steed under the command

of what the soul has seen and is able to remember. Which brings us round
to the whole reason for telling this myth. That is, to highlight that dreams,
while being initiatory, are at the same time, prophetic. In other words, we
are being loved slowly forward; we are being remembered into who we
are really, based on what the soul saw."

⁓

"I get quite frustrated," says the man next to me. "I just can't seem to
remember my dreams anymore. Weeks, even months, go by and all I
can remember are little flashes, less than any of the dreams recounted
here today," he says. "Just like a 'pop' here and a 'pop' there. Tiny
little flashes."

"Me, too," I shrug. "That is, from time to time, weeks even
months go by. But be reminded that it's not the content of dreams that
is important, for, doesn't it seem that we are always looking for ways
to strip-mine the psyche? Aren't we always looking at dreams for what
they are trying to tell us about ourselves? No wonder the dreams dry up!
They're trying to resist all of our many and smarmy ego advances.

"But now images like those you've just described come along
like this, 'pop,'" I say, making Bob Fosse hands, "and 'pop,' because
they're trying to show us what's essentially important, that is, that
we're illuminated, lit-from-within beings of light. But it's all too easy
to miss this if all we're doing is strip-mining dreams for the content
of what they can give us, or for how we can apply them to our lives or
whatever. Remember, the medicine of the dreamtime *is* the dreamtime.
It's dreaming per se. So when we cannot remember the contents of our
dreams, it's because the medicine is being applied directly.

"It was our old dream friend Freud, you may recall, who said that
the 'function of dreams is as a guardian of sleep.' But if the function of
dreams is as a guardian of sleep, is not the obverse is also true? Is not the

function of sleep also as a guardian of dreams? For the ancient Greeks, sleep and death are twin brothers. So it's our nightly bodily dying that is important, essential, and restorative because it allows the light of our being—that light from whence we came and to which we are returning—to shine through us in the dark of dreams."

"I so need to be reminded of this," he shakes his head.

"We all do. There's a gal I work with in prison and every time I'm out there she asks me to remind her that she is a being of light. Just this, every single time. So when we cannot remember the dreams that have been entrusted to our care while sleeping, the task it to look around to the dreams that are being entrusted to our waking care—and to develop the eye of the heart so that we might begin to see the imaginal light behind these waking dreams. We don't have to look very far; the dream of the world—*Earth Dreaming*—is quite dying for our participation."

"So we needn't take dreaming so literally?"

"Well, the whole point of working this way is to discover, in an ongoing way, that the whole thing is dreaming. So look around for an image that grabs your heart's eye and dream with it, that is, dream it out into the world again, only mixed with your being—your heartfelt and dreaming participation in it now."

"But there's also a way that you have," one of the dreamers says then, "of remembering dreams from waaaaaay back," she reaches her arm behind her head. "Dreams that, well . . . that even the dreamers themselves have forgotten."

"I work with a fellow who says that his memory is so bad that he could easily be like that guy in *Groundhog Day*, bringing in the same dream to me week after week," I chuckle. "Ah, but now memory, that is, as we moderns commonly think of it, has nothing to do with it. For when we're in the imaginal realm, that interactive field of dreams, we don't need to 'remember' any images. All we have to do is look over and see the images, see what's there. This is what I mean when I say that dreams are trying to teach us their wisdom. It's not like we have to ask, 'Oh, what was that dream?'" I rub my fingers together then to make as though I'm fingering through dream files. "No, we know that this image and that image belong together, and that this dream and that dream are connected, because the images announce their connections by stepping forward out of the otherwise discreet shadows. They step forward, or pop up."

"So the only thing that you're doing, in fact, is noticing this, seeing it when it happens, and letting us all in on it."

"As a way of inviting you to develop these capacities," I nod. "Or that's my sincere hope, at least. So that by coming to a genuine love of images you will begin to feel your way into the heart as an organ of perception, to develop imaginally thinking hearts and the corresponding theophanic vision. So that the Burning Bush is experienced as something more than just a brushfire. If, as the Sufis suggest, each of us gets the God we are capable of, then this work strives to make us ever more capable of the Gods of our Being, those Gods that we came here to remember and display.

"And as long as we can feel the connections, that is, experience them directly when we open up the dreams, we're well on our way. It's a bit like Eliza Doolittle complaining to Professor Higgins in beginning of *Pygmalion* that she can't talk all 'genteel-like' the way he does. And then he comes back with something like, 'Nonsense, girl, if you can hear the difference in the phonetic sounds, you're halfway to making them.'"

"So you think it's developable? That everyone has this capacity?"

"If I didn't, I wouldn't be in this line of work," I smile expansively. "But perhaps I should add here that I take the *connections between things as an absolute given*. So you'll likewise want to start with this as a premise. In other words, learn to take it on faith that everything is, indeed, connected. And perhaps from there it's merely a matter of noticing how, in what ways."

Then, "You may recall that the Goddess Memory, or Mnemosyne, as she was known to the Greeks, was one of the Titans. She was a daughter, therefore, of the first generation of deities, of Ouranos and Gaia. And she was also the mother of the Muses, who were conceived when she slept with Zeus for nine consecutive nights."

"Who are the nine Muses again?"

"I can't remember," I deadpan. Then, "Oh, and of course you'd ask that! I don't honestly remember. Google them," I suggest. "The point is that in Hesiod's *Theogony*, kings and poets alike receive their powers of speech from the special relationship they have with Mnemosyne and her daughters. So what does this tell us?"

"That memory is much more closely related to the arts than we imagine it to be."

"Yes. And now the thing about the Goddess Memory is that her memory doesn't just run one way. In other words, her memory is not solely dedicated to the past, as it commonly is with us. It's also directed to what we think of as the future. So it has both a fated strand that is threaded to the past and a destiny strand that is threaded to, and indeed pulled along by, the future. So when we endeavor to remember dream images this way, what soon becomes evident is that we are likewise being remembered forward by the dream of the world."

"So it's that exchange again."

"And the more we participate in this exchange, feeling our way into it, the more we begin to notice two things. First, that once an image penetrates the heart, it stays there."

"So we don't have to keep putting it there over and over, for example, like we do when we're trying to memorize the multiplication table in the second grade, and the brain doesn't seem to want to cooperate," someone offers.

"The images that either enter the heart realm on their own accord, in other words, those that penetrate us directly, as well as those we place there intentionally, linger in our hearts, waiting, just waiting to be noticed whenever we turn our attention toward them."

"I noticed that as soon as you reminded me of slapping my cat," the dreamer says, gently padding at her heart. "It's right here."

"Isn't this because, despite the appearance of its muscular mass, the secret of the heart's effectiveness is that it's hollow? It's this hollowness of our hearts that provides a perfect meeting place within us—between the dream of our bodies and the uncivilized and instinctive stories that are written there, and our personal presence, as that which attends. But at the same time, the heart also acts as the meeting place between us and the presence of the Other," I pause. "Though, perhaps it should be added here that we need to practice turning our attention to the heart realm in order to notice this, in order to become present to the Presence.

"But now the second thing that we begin to experience in this exchange," I continue, "is the longing that's coming from the other side. So, for example, in your Whimpering Creature dream, what you, and now everyone else can feel so strongly, is the longing that's coming through the Whimpering Creature from the soul/spirit realms."

"So our human participation, however paltry, matters?"

"However stumbling along in the dark it might feel like to us, it is received by those on the other side—by dream images as well as the ancestors—as the ongoing gift that we offer their being," I say.

"So is it like the longing you felt coming from those little puzzles in your neighbor's toy box?"

I nod.

"Are you saying, then, that without our participation that even the ancestors would cease to be?"

"I'm saying that they would cease to be *this* way, the way that they can be in the world through us." Then, "Perhaps this is how the ancestors offer themselves as spiritual agents? And maybe this is why there's what's known as a 'family fate'?"

"Because some things take longer than one generation to work through?"

"It's certainly a story worth considering. So, yes, for some images, the Jeremy Dreaming image, for example, who hangs out here in my office—he would cease to be altogether, except perhaps as an artifact of dreaming—the once dreamt—were it not for the ongoing feeling-into-being exchange between us."

Part III:

Dreams as Destiny

What is Being Asked of Us Now?

What is the dream of a dream-book-being, shaping itself between dreamers in the dark? Feeling our way along, perhaps it can only be seen, recognized, when finally, it *is*, when at long last it is remembered into being? And perhaps this is why the dreams keep dreaming, nagging now to be included? Noticing a common dream thread between these nagging dreams, and feeling as though a place must somehow be created for them, giving them another place to be, the following dream arrives:

A single-file line of people winds as far back as the eye can see, all the way to the distant horizon and presumably beyond. It is not clear in which direction this line is moving, but all those gathered are receiving and being received by me. As the line likewise carries on behind me as far as the eye can see in the opposite direction, it suggests that there is far more going on than just what I'm personally experiencing, and that there are others who are perhaps receiving and being received in various places along this Underworld receiving line.

As each being is being received by the other, there is deep bowing between us, as if to say, "I see you. Thank you very much for being here and for coming to pay your respect," though no words are actually spoken; the entire exchange is a gesturing.

A sandy-haired woman and I bow to one another. Then I see a set of twins, and, as we bow to each other, I am filled with curiosity, wondering if they were lucky enough to die together. The twins smile then, to confirm that, just as they were lucky enough to be born into the world together, they were also lucky enough to die together.

Perhaps this is what's being asked of us now? Perhaps it's through similarly reverent gestures in Underworld Receiving Lines that we might finally begin to experience Rilke's "Church in the East" at the supper table, with the children, and inside the dishes and glasses? As the following dream seems to suggest, maybe it's the so-called dead who can uniquely teach us to see, really see, so that with them, and through them, we learn to stop focusing on the material surface of things and we begin to see the radiant light of ensouled being.

ELL & ELL(Y) DREAMING

"We are putting our home on the market," begins the dreamer. "Outside in our backyard, a group of inspectors inspects things, going through everything and moving things around, making their notes and so forth, so that we can get the house in order to sell."

"Your waking-world home?"

"Yes and no," she answers. "It has the feel of our waking-world home but the backyard looks nothing at all like our backyard. And my husband and I are out there watching the inspectors. I'm somewhat disgruntled by the disheveled mess these guys are making. They've moved a little footbridge, for example, to check around it, but when they are through making their notes, they don't bother to move it back. So my husband and I walk back over there to right things again. But that's when we notice a good-sized hole in the ground.

"And suddenly there's a strong light poking through the clouds and shining directly down into this hole, rather like a beam of light from a flashlight in heaven. As we peer into the hole, the light illuminates things so that we can see that it goes way, way, way down. And I'm like," she bends to show us how she peers down the hole, "'Whoa!'" she says, reeling back. "And my husband turns to me then and says, 'This must be the hole of that badger we saw, huh?'

"And immediately the image of a badger flashes upon the screen of my mind. But then I'm confused. I am not sure if this is the badger that 'we' saw, or if it's just the badger that popped into my mind when my husband said the word 'badger,'" she shrugs. "In other words, I'm not even sure I saw the badger that my husband is referring to when he says 'that badger we saw.' I don't remember if I ever even saw that badger, or if this is a memory of that badger that I'm seeing, or if this is just some 'picture' of badger that imaged its way into my consciousness.

"But then there's a jump cut. And we're back inside the house now. The badger confusion is still very much 'badgering' me . . . when I pick up a magazine that came with the morning paper and discover that the cover story is about a town that's been abandoned down in the South, in a place like Tennessee, or Arkansas.

"So I turn inside to find the story. I see a number of full-page pictures then of the various houses that people have just walked away from. And as I read, I discover that the town was originally built around some kind of industry, one in particular, though I don't remember what that industry is now. The article talked about it and talked too about when that industry shut down its factory. There was simply no work for the town's population anymore and everyone was forced then to move away.

"But what is so remarkable about this particular town," she continues, "is that folks left all of their belongings behind, as though they just up and walked away. So the entire town is stuck, really, in what seems like a moment of time, rather like it would be in a photograph, only the entire town is now like a living, stuck-in-a-moment-of-time photograph. A real ghost town.

"And so, naturally, the photographs featured in the article capture this feeling of being stuck-in-a-moment particularly well. And what really catches my attention then, is one house in particular, one that doesn't seem. . . very well-suited to the South. In other words, it's more like something you'd find out here in California. So I'm looking at it rather intently and noticing all of the architectural details, the columns and so forth, and the courtyard. It reminds me of something that might have been built in the 70s, something that you'd find in the Hollywood Hills, say, or Topanga Canyon.

"And I turn the page then to discover that the next picture in the series is of the interior of this very same home that has caught my attention. The photograph is from the foyer looking toward the dining room. And as I peer into the photograph, I notice that there is a stack of dishes on the sideboard that looks . . . very . . . familiar. I peer at it intently and think, 'Hey, I used to have that very same set of china.' Then, 'I *loved* that set of china.'

"And no sooner do I remember this, than I find myself transported into the actual dining room in the photograph. And, filled with a kind of amazement, I wander around slowly then, carefully and delicately, noticing things and gently touching them, completely marveling at the place and the fact that I'm here. Then I pick up one of the plates from the set of china, and I'm completely thrown back to a time when I had this exact pattern. It was right after my husband and I got married. I really loved this particular pattern then, and, holding it, I find that I do still—it's sweet and hopeful, cheerful even—patterned all over, in a primitive style, with tiny, dabbed-red flowers. And just seeing this set of china in the dining room of this house makes me happy, filled with tenderness, and a kind of wonder that seems to hold a promise of sorts for the future.

"And then I think, 'Well, why couldn't we just live here?' I gaze around and imagine what it would be like to just move our entire family to live in this house, and as I continue to imagine the possibility of this, I wander slowly toward what turns out to be the kitchen.

"When I enter the kitchen," the dreamer continues, "what I notice first is that there is a half-eaten snack, complete with cracker crumbs and bits of cheese sitting on the countertop, and now a line of ants that lead up to it, as though whoever left this place left it mid-snack.

"And as I continue walking through the kitchen, what I notice next is a sign on the tile of the countertop, where someone has taken an indelible black marker and written:

Ell & Ell(y)
were happy here!

across several of the cream-colored tiles. I am really taken with this message, as though it was written by either Ell or Ell(y) for someone just like me to find."

A silence enters the room with this image. Noticing this, those gathered try to give it enough room to be.

"In other words, it seems purposive?" I ask after a time.

She nods. "And I'm noticing the handwriting itself . . . you know, in that way that handwriting is so incredibly personal? So I'm noticing the handwriting and thinking about the quality, the manner of the writing itself—for it clearly comes from an era when penmanship mattered—it's almost like calligraphy . . . and I'm thinking about the message, too, that is, that Ell and Ell(y) were happy here! when I notice a bit further down the countertop that there is dishwater in the sink, and that it still has some of its soapy bubbles! So I stick my hand in the dishwater only to discover that it's still warm! As though Ell and Ell(y) left half-way through a cheese and cracker snack and before they even got a chance to drain the recently-used dirty dishwater. They did take last-minute time, however, to write that note for whoever might come along after and find it. And I'm really, very deeply struck by this," she says.

"Then I turn to see that, on a perpendicular countertop, there is a bunch of fresh roses. But instead of being in a vase, it's as though they're in an envelope, as though it's some kind of container to keep them fresh and together, and, though they are laying down—as though they've just arrived in the mail or something—there is no water leaking out of the envelope that holds them. And, telling it like this, I realize that . . . it doesn't make much waking-world sense, the way I'm describing the plastic envelope thing now, but it made complete and clever sense in the dreamtime. Like, 'That's an intriguing and nifty little invention.'

"And moving along through the kitchen then, I turn to see what's in the fridge. I open the door to discover that there is fresh food inside, all kinds of it. But this is when my son's alarm goes off and I wake up. And, oh! I am so disappointed and really frustrated by the alarm going off precisely then . . ."

"Because?"

"Because I want to know more about Ell and Ell(y)," she says, in a tone that suggests it should be obvious. "Like who are they and what happened to them?"

"Is there the sense that they are in the dream house?"

"As presences," she says. "I'm not concerned, in other words, that one of them will come upon me and demand to know what I am doing there, or anything like that. No. In fact, it's as though they are expecting someone. And there is a very strong and lingering sense of their being there, only not in substantial bodies."

"So, in spirit?"

"Yes," the dreamer nods.

"Well, okay," I take a deep breath, as the images manage to settle. "Let's see if we can feel our way into some of these questions you're so curious about by entering the dreamscape together."

As is our practice then, I instruct the dreamer to notice what she notices and to let the rest of us in on it as I repeat the dream back to her. "So what pops up for you?" I ask when the retelling is complete.

"Well, the whole opening sequence seems to belong to a different dream," she says. "I notice that."

"Um-hum. Anything else?"

"Well, the house, of course. The sweet pattern of the china set that I remember, actually, as having in the waking-world, long ago when I was first married. But mostly, and overarchingly, it's the moment-in-time aspect of things—like the time sequence in the kitchen and how it progresses with the half-eaten cracker on the countertop and the line of ants that have found their way to it now, the handwritten note scribbled indelibly onto the tiles of the countertop, the lukewarm dishwater, the roses that have so recently arrived, and all the fresh food in the fridge."

"It seems to suggest that they didn't know they'd be leaving anytime soon."

"And it all seems so eerie," she nods, "as though I have just missed Ell and Ell(y) by the smallest fraction of a second," she holds up her thumb and forefinger indicating the smallest of spaces, "by the turn of a head, or the blink of an eye, or when I stopped on the other side, for just a few seconds to look at that photograph of the outside of their house. As though they were just here, half of a cheese cracker ago, or when there were still some dirty dishes in the sink, and . . . though I know that's not really true because the photographer had to take the picture for the article in the first place, that's absolutely what it feels like . . . so I'm really, really struck by the moment-in-time of Ell and Ell(y) leaving," she continues then, "as though it's really just . . . a . . . moment in time, but that moment just keeps happening, and nothing changes, I mean, nothing *really* changes, except Ell and Ell(y) are no longer in living bodies."

"Because they're on the other side of being?"

"That's what it feels like, yes." Then, "It makes me think of my mother. Maybe because we're coming up to the one-year anniversary of her death," she shrugs, "and it makes me think of . . . her death, and my father's death, my own . . . death, death in general."

There is a long silence then, which allows the presence of Death a place in the room.

"And so you imagine that Ell and Ell(y) wrote that note hurriedly, as in the-last-thing-they-could-do-before-passing-over-to-the-spiritual-realm for all those who might come after and wonder about such things, or perhaps wonder about them?"

"That's what it feels like. But it also feels as though they knew it would be me specifically. Or if not me, then someone a lot like me. Someone, for example, who might also find passage here through one of the details, like that memory of the china pattern. Because it seems that it was my noticing that, which, in effect, teleported me into the actual dining room. And so it strikes me that this connectedness between us, this love that we have for the same china pattern is a kind of portal. And that for others it might be different, the sideboard, for example, or the dining room table and chairs, or . . . I don't know. Or . . . maybe not, maybe the 'key' to getting teleported to the inside of Ell and Ell(y)'s home has everything to do with sharing a love for that particular pattern? For it seems as though it's truly the shared love that we have that not only drew me to the photograph, but once I remembered having that pattern myself, and loving it, I was allowed passage . . . and I was transported then to the actual home of Ell and Ell(y) in Tennessee, or Arkansas, or 'down yonder' in the South wherever, through the portal of that photograph in the magazine."

"So shared love of a particular pattern is key?"

"Shared love of a particular pattern," she repeats slowly as though tasting her words, "does seem key, yes," she nods. There is a long silence then as those gathered attempt to hold what the dreamer has just said.

Then, "And the other thing that really pops up for me," she continues, "is the profound disappointment I experience upon awakening. I actually got angry with my son and the fact that he'd set that alarm so that he would wake up in time to get to school!" she laughs. "And I tried to go back to sleep afterwards, to see if I could re-enter the sleeping dream, but . . ." she trails off.

"So the unexpected waking awakens your frustration and your curiosity?"

"And my longing to go back there."

"Okay," I say. "But now, we want to include the unexpected awakening, the anger and frustration toward your son, your curiosity, and your longing to go back, as equal parts of the dream."

She lets out a sigh. "I'm angry with my son a lot lately," she says, flashing a big grin.

"We'll get to that. And we'll see if we can go back to Ell and Ell(y)'s. But first, let's get a little curious about that opening sequence, the prelude, as it were."

"They don't seem at all connected. But we've been doing this together long enough that I know better," she smiles.

"Well, let's see what we can notice, if anything," I suggest. "So . . . you and your husband are getting ready to put your house on the market. And, though the house has the 'feel' of your waking-world house, it does not look like your house."

"Can I ask a quick question about houses?" someone asks, turning tentatively toward the dreamer as though asking permission. Then, "Why there are so many different houses in dreams? And why are they so infrequently of the houses in which we actually live in the waking-world?"

"Marvelous, isn't it? All the different houses in the dreamtime? And they're all over the place. With friends and lovers, indeed, whole towns of people who seem to know us. Who *are* all those people?" I ask.

"Well, now because folks so frequently dream of being in a house— whether it's their waking-world house, the house they grew up in, someone else's house, or different houses that are very much 'theirs' in a felt-sense . . . though they resemble little of the actual places in which they dwell in the waking-world, or even when they mostly do but they are somehow still 'different'—the question, 'what does house mean?' gets asked a great deal.

"It's important, however, to have an imaginal sense of 'house' as 'that which psychically contains me'—'me,' that is, as the dreamer— not just the lit-up and easily recognized 'I' of the dream, but the sleeping un-lit side, too. Dreams endeavor to move us constantly into the enduring and unbreakable unity of these twofold sides of being in creation, in the context of the world. Therefore, one of the reasons that we find ourselves in so many different dream houses is because 'that which psychically contains me' is always changing, just as we're always changing. So even though the house we go to sleep in is the same house we wake up in (unless there's been an earthquake or some such thing), the dreamer who wakes up merely appears to be the very same individual who went to sleep the night before because, of course, we are always and ever changing—even if the only 'evidence' we have of this is that we're getting older, that is, we're moving one day closer to our eventual deaths. And it's the ever-changing houses of our dreams, as 'that which psychically contains me,' that remind us of this open secret. So the various houses we find ourselves in are trying to keep us from imagining that we know ourselves," I suggest, "by drawing us ever deeper into the mystery of Mystical Poverty."

"I'm sorry," the questioner says then, looking over at the dreamer with an expression that asks for continuing patience. "I'm . . . confused. When you ask, 'Who are all those people in the dreamtime?' what I think I'm hearing you say is that these images, like Jeremy Dreaming, are of the dead."

"Well, they're not only of the dead," I say. "What we're practicing when we gather like this has everything to do with moving into relationship with ourselves, with each other, with images, with the dead, with the divine, and the whole of the world by moving us into Mystical Poverty. So it's not to be taken too literally. It's not another theory—or something that can be verified objectively. In other words, it's not an invitation to go pouring through the records to see if there is an actual town down South that is now a ghost town, with a home in it that looks just like the one in this dream. What we're practicing here is a mythological orientation. So these are not dreams that have happened. Instead, as this particular dream suggests rather strikingly, they are always happening."

"So we're not going to find an obituary in a Tennessee newspaper archive for Ell and Ell(y)?"

"Ell and Ell(y) are dream beings who, without bodies of their own, look upon us over here in the land of the 'living living,' still very much in our own incarnating bodies, and say, 'I've got kin in that body,' just as in that marvelous poem by Hafiz:

> Plant
> So that your own heart
> Will grow.
>
> Love
> So God will think,
>
> "Ahhhhhhh,
> I got kin in that body!

I should start inviting that soul over
For coffee and
Rolls."

Sing
Because this is a food
Our starving world
Needs.

Laugh
Because that is the purest
Sound.[17]

"Plant, instructs Hafiz, so that your own heart will grow. In other words, the task is to begin the work of your life. So begin doing what you're already doing as a practice for being, with love and through the heart as an organ of perception, and you will undoubtedly attract the divine as epiphanized presences that will want to lend themselves to your unfolding project in the world, to what you are planting.

"And sometimes these epiphanized forms will come as images in dreams and sometimes they will come as waking-world presences, or, when they are of the so-called 'actual' dead like Jeremy Dreaming, perhaps both.

"Additionally," I continue, "whenever there is an affinity, that is, a shared imagination between what we came here to remember and display and what the so-called dead came here to remember and display and didn't quite finish while they were still in their own living bodies, well . . . it seems that they get very, very interested in us and in sharing our bodies, because . . . well, maybe it's the only way to realize their unfinished work? In other words, they seem to want to help us, with how we're doing what we're already doing, through our living bodies."

"So we're in the same spiritual soul clan, so to speak?"

"Well, it's a good story," I shrug. "And so recognizing this, spiritual soul beings lend themselves to our projects, that is, to the project of who we are becoming for the sake of the whole world and the Earth's spiritual unfolding."

"Okay," the questioner says, "but then what's the difference between these images of the so-called dead, I mean, imaginally speaking, and say, my husband, or my daughter—who both showed up last night in my dreams?"

"Well, from the dream's perspective, nothing. But in terms of the images themselves . . . well, it's not really your husband in the dream and it's not really your daughter, right? Just as it's not really you. The dreamtime merely uses your husband, and your daughter, and 'you' as familiars to help you—you, that is, as the dreamer—see the story and keep it all within a certain close and unfolding context." Then, "But so long as your husband is in a body, that is, as long as he is incarnating into the world of the 'living living,' we have to imagine that he has his own project, just like you or me or any one of us."

"So he likewise has that which he came here to remember and display?"

"And your daughter, too. They are both still very much involved in the stuff of spiritual soul being worked with in and through their own incarnating, living bodies. On the other hand, those images that so generously lend themselves to the project of our lives each night, those images that we do not recognize except in a dreaming way, well, we might want to imagine that ours are the only physical bodies to which they have access. In other words, it is only through us that they can become spiritual forces in the world at all."

"So they are trying to continue on with what they came here to remember and display through us, through our bodies and lives?"

"And through our unique and heartfelt attention to their being," I nod. "Because they recognize the 'shared imagination' of the projects in which we're involved. But by 'project' we don't want to imagine that

it's the particular projects we 'do.' 'Project' here refers instead to the
project of life, to the art and practice of becoming who we are really, and
those 'patterns' that we share," I turn to the dreamer to highlight the
significance of the pattern she shares with Ell and Ell(y).

"So by recognizing an individual 'body' for accomplishing this, or
at least accomplishing it further in the world, image beings show up in
our dreams to help us along. The task for us, therefore, is to move into
relationship with what is between us," I pause. Then, "Does this answer
your question?"

"So the difference lies in whether or not the images have
corresponding material bodies? In other words, without living bodies,
those beings on the other side, like my father, for example, who died
many years ago now, can only do their 'work,' if at all, through our being,
through our bodies here on this side?"

"And our careful tending," I nod.

"So it's ancestral?"

"Yes, so long as 'ancestral' is not taken literally to mean 'blood lines.'
Imaginally, 'ancestral' means that we have a shared imagination—that
we belong to the same spiritual thread of being. So I can speak of that
oak, for example, right there," I say, indicating the large tree on our front
lawn, "as one of the Grandmothers. And obviously she is, substantially
speaking, a tree, so we don't share the same blood lines, the same
inherited DNA in a materially measureable sort of way, but we, that is,
Oak and our family, nonetheless recognize each another as beings from
the same soul/spirit clan. She lends herself to our family's shared project
by opening her arms and heart in the way that she receives us, in the way
she looks out for us. Meanwhile, we make offerings to her that say 'thank
you' and 'I see you,' and from time to time we lay our worries at her feet.
We perform ritual around her. And though we try to listen to her

concerns, I must admit we tend to take more than we give, so we neglect listening to her deeply enough.

"But now it's not only her, that is, as tree, to whom we are making offerings. She is the material oak of Spiritual Oak Being, so she is at the same time the Grandmothers Dreaming," I pause. Then, "Does this help?"

"Thank you," the questioner says, then, "yes," she adds, as she turns to nod at the dreamer as if to let her know that she is through asking questions for the time being.

"Okay," I say, turning to the dreamer. "Where were we?"

"Going into the backyard," the dreamer says, "which is quite different than our waking-world backyard."

"How so?"

"Well, there's nothing growing in the dream yard, for one thing. It's set against a steep slope, just as ours is, but in the dream there's a giant . . . pine tree . . . in the far back corner that keeps almost the whole yard in perpetual shade, so nothing can really grow. And there's a kind of wet, spongy-ness to the ground, as though there's a bit of a drainage problem or . . . maybe it's just wet because so little sun reaches under the branches of that pine? I don't know," she says, "but it's really not a whole heck of a lot like our backyard."

"A reminder, again, to not take the dream too literally," I suggest.

"So I shouldn't be searching around for another set of that particular china on eBay?" she asks, smiling broadly then as everyone laughs.

"Well, it's not that you shouldn't do that, you absolutely can. But we wouldn't want to mistake this for soul-making. Buying those particular dishes and keeping them around might be a way to remind yourself in an ongoing, everyday kind of way of what you really love. But all too often we fall into the trap of thinking it's the things themselves— we become transfixed by the things instead of looking for the light that's shining through them. So seeing the pattern in china that you use every day to help you remember the love that you and Ell and Ell(y) share, might, in effect, transport you to their dining room and kitchen, but remembering the pattern on that china and entering it imaginally ought to get you there too, and you will be developing imaginal capacities of soul, along with the will to practice these capacities, at the very same time."

"Yeah," the dreamer nods, "and I tend toward the literal so I need to be mindful of this."

"We all do. But this is the difference between idol and icon." Then, "And the unfamiliar backyard reminds us that we're entering unfamiliar territory. And this is beautifully rendered in the dream when you are transported into that dining room and wander around in a state of wonder and discovery. This is what the dreamtime is actually after—moving us out of a closed system and into an open one of perpetual wonder and discovery. But, as you already know, when we buy the dishes and have them around, we wonder at them, and discover them for a time—until the love affair between us seems to wane and we start looking around for another set of china to wonder at and marvel over. The newness of things invites a kind of discovery between us, but when the newness wears off, we fall out of relationship, and that same set of china is reduced by us then into 'things' that need replacing by us, but only so that we might again experience the wonder and discovery of relationship.

"We do this to one another as well, that is, each and every time we approach the other as someone we already 'know' instead of as a being through whom we can move into an ongoing relationship of wonder and discovery.

"Yet now, as you yourself can so strongly feel, the intensification of your being as you are transported into that dining room of discovery, is precisely what the dream is highlighting for you. And as you move through that dining room, at the same time you move into your own open and generous, giving personhood, and you are filled with a kind of wonder of discovery. But . . . we're getting ahead of ourselves here and so let's go back to that back yard and ask . . . what do you make of those inspectors?"

"Well, there are three or four of them, and they're just doing that typical inspecting thing," she answers. "But what strikes me about what they're doing is the way things are getting moved around."

"Things that would otherwise not get moved?"

"Even though it irks me that they're doing this," she nods.

"Because you want things to stay just the way they are?"

"Always," she chuckles. "I'm pretty much resistant to all change unless I'm the one instigating it." Several people laugh, recognizing this tendency in themselves.

"But it's through this moving around of things that would otherwise not be moved around that you notice . . . what?"

"That deep hole in the ground."

"And so you go over to take a closer look. And what do you notice then?"

"Well, that light streaming through the clouds, shining directly into the hole and illuminating the 'whole.'"

"That's hole with an 'h' and whole with a 'wh'—the 'whole hole?'"

"Yes. And the pun seems intended. There is the sense that this light is trying to illuminate the whole hole, as though it's trying to lift the veil between what—under 'normal' circumstances—is hidden from plain view, that now—because of the inspector movement and that light shining down—is being revealed."

"Um-hum. And what's that?" I ask.

"Well, first of all that there's a hole there at all. It's clearly been there but . . . who knew?" she shrugs. "And secondly, that the hole goes way, way, *way* deeper down than I ever could have imagined. It causes me to reel back when I look down into it. Like 'Whoa!'" She mimes reeling back. "And the ground underneath is wet and spongy, too," she adds. "So it all makes me a little queasy."

Though it's always important to make our way slowly in the dreamtime, it's important to slow down even more when the dreamer's reaction is so fully embodied. By allowing this extra room around the images and the dreamer, we endeavor to hold the imaginal space and, in a sense, stretch it out. This way the dream images and the dreamer are given the proper space, that is, space that is held and contained, so that within this held, communal space they can find the imaginal freedom required to make their way "organically" towards what's trying to "be" between them.

"And that's when your husband suggests that this must be the hole of the badger that the two of you saw," I prompt her after a time.

"And 'Badger' appears as an image, clear as a sunny day, but that's when I become quite confused. I still don't know if I saw that badger with my husband," she shrugs.

"And why, do you imagine, does this matter?"

"Well . . . because I can't tell if it really happened or not. I can't tell if I really saw that badger with my husband as he says I did, or if this badger is just some generic badger that popped into my mind, or . . ."

"Yes, you are quite clear in your confusion," I agree, "when you first told us this part of the dream, and again now, but . . . why does it matter if 'Badger' is this badger or that?"

She thinks about this. "It's a question of reality," she says then, quite simply. "What is 'real?' What's *reality*?"

"And what strikes you now, if anything, about what's 'real?'"

"That they both are," she sighs. "But I get caught in my head all the time, thinking that it has to be one way or the other."

"Once we move into the heart and its expansive thinking/feeling space, what we begin to notice is that there's plenty of room for all of it to be 'real,' whether images are experienced in the substantial realm of things, or in the essential realm of things, or both. The only 'real' difference lies in the 'form' of the image; one is material, while the other 'having no physical substance,' is immaterial, which is what the word 'immaterial' originally meant."

"It's easy," the dreamer says then, "to see the preference we moderns have for the 'material' realm when we note that the word 'immaterial' has come to mean 'unimportant,' and 'having no consequence.'"

"'This sense has crept into the conversation and writings of barbarians,' notes Samuel Johnson in his most famous dictionary, 'but,' he goes on to say, it 'ought to be utterly rejected.'"

"In an interview I read several years ago now," the dreamer offers, "the president of Johns Hopkins said that because the school is so rooted in the scientific method, it's not providing a sense of values to its students. So Johns Hopkins, and other schools like it, have the potential for turning out what he referred to as 'highly skilled barbarians,'" she pauses. "With so much emphasis on 'objective knowing,'" she shakes her head, "on public information that can be verified, I'm . . . having trouble with knowing what I know. Or with accepting what I don't know," she shrugs. "Or even that I know or don't know . . . and it . . . bothers me that there's anything I don't know. I want to just look it up—Google it—and then add it to the files of what I know."

"So what presents itself as a personal struggle in your dream—*Did that actually happen or did I just imagine it?*—is a reflection of the current struggle we find ourselves in culturally, that is, collectively, and the rest of the dream tumbles out of this general state of confusion."

"And all the stuff that unfolds in the house seems to suggest that things don't just happen in a historical sense," the dreamer adds, "at least not in the way we think of history as having a familiar beginning, middle, and end. But it's more than 'just' something that we imagine, too. In the dream, it's as though everything is happening all at once."

"In other words, it's always happening?"

"Yes," she nods. "And that's the thing . . . that . . . most strikes me still—the all-at-once-ness of the dream. I mean . . . I know that I couldn't have gotten there any sooner than I did . . ."

"Because there is no 'sooner?'"

"Exactly," she says. "But the intellectual knowing of this does not in any way hinder the bodily desire for it to be otherwise. I want so much to know these women, and not just to learn about them, and what happened to them, but . . . more, much more . . ." she trails off.

"Okay," I say, after a time. "Then there's no need to wait any longer. Can you remember that china pattern, those wee all-over flowers . . ."

"Dabbed all-over red flowers," the dreamer says, "tiny, and in a primitive style."

"So are you able to picture those promising little flowers, to feel your way into them?"

She nods.

"And can you allow them now to do their transporting work?"

She nods again.

Then, "Can you feel the all-at-once-ness of Ell and Ell(y)'s place?"

"I'm there. Inside. And it's actually palpable. As though I am being touched all over by it."

We want to wait here, as the dreamer moves deeper into the being-ness that the dream home offers. Then, "And what, if anything, do you notice now?"

"Well, it feels as though the home has been left for me, specifically, that it's being entrusted to my care. As if I am being asked to return here on a regular basis to check in on things, to clean up those cracker crumbs, for example, and to get rid of the ants, to drain the dishwater, put the china away in the sideboard and . . . to generally care for the place."

"As a caretaker would?"

"A loving caretaker, yes."

"So it's not about doing the chores?"

"There are light housekeeping duties. But it's not that kind of care that's being asked of me, really . . . it seems more like the care of being in a place that once belonged to Ell and Ell(y), living there, or at least companioning their home in an imaginal and embodied way, loving it and caring for it in a way that Ell and Ell(y) no longer can."

"Because they are no longer in bodies?"

She nods.

"And is this something you're interested in taking on?"

She nods again. "Well, Ell and Ell(y) seem to have written the note on the tile specifically for me, knowing that it would be me who would find it."

"So they picked you?"

"Yes, and even though I know that I can never really know why they picked me . . . I mean, why did I pick my husband?" she shrugs. "Why did he pick me? Even after more than thirty years of marriage, the reasons are not altogether clear," she smiles. "So it's not really that I want to know why they picked me . . . but I would like to know what it is they see in me."

"Do you have any inkling?"

"What I feel very strongly in their message is that they were really, really happy living in this home, in this world, in their lives, together . . . as though they . . . *flourished* . . . and that this is somehow supposed to be a message for me, specifically," she says, as the emotion begins to take her. "It's like they want me to know what's possible. Because . . . well, it seems that there's a way to flourish, to be like them, and they . . ." she trails off.

" . . . See something in you that makes them think you could flourish?"

She nods. "And I want to flourish. And being in their home . . . I don't know . . . it's as though I can, it cheers me on, encourages me, and it's as though they are, too . . ."

"Ell and Ell(y)?"

"Even though I don't know them, and they don't know me, or at least not in the waking-world of things . . . but I can immediately sense the possibilities for our shared imagination and the depth of the experiment."

"Aristotle has a marvelous word for flourishing: *eudaimonia,* which suggests that flourishing means 'in harmony with the daimon,' in harmonious being with the soul-twin, with the 'pattern' that, together with the soul-twin, we have chosen to live out and through in this incarnation."

"So recognizing the pattern *is* key," the dreamer offers. "Actually."

"Whether or not the thing you love is in your hands, as in that set of china that you're sniffing around for on eBay, or an imaginal pattern that you carry within, or both. What matters, actually, is not the china so much as it is the love that draws you to that pattern. In other words, it's the light behind the pattern and what this brings you to."

"Ell and Ell(y)'s."

"Yes, but not in an 'over there' kind of way. Ell and Ell(y)'s is an ongoing orientation to being. Within. You. *You* are Ell and Ell(y)'s. You are their home. You have been entrusted to your care (and theirs). And not just the lit-up part of you that is already familiar to you, but 'you' in Mystical Poverty, as a twofold being. The image of Ell and Ell(y)'s merely helps you see this, to know it, to experience it as 'actual,' as a place in which to be. And it's the all-at-once-ness of the image that offers itself to your imagination, as a vivid and loving, place-being-held-for-you-in-the-world kind of way. So you'll want to keep going back to this living body place, keep going back to what you love, and to the possibilities that this love offers to you and for you, because it's this love, specifically, in this place that is being held for you, that is trying to remember you forward, out into the world, because . . . well, it turns out it wants something from you."

The dreamer turns to look at me with an air of expectation.

"Your flourishing."

"I was hoping that you were going to say 'art,'" the dreamer confesses.

"Well, what if I did?"

"Then I'd drop everything and do art," she says. "I'd give myself permission to call myself an artist and . . . I'd make art."

"Why aren't you calling yourself an artist already?"

"Because . . . I'm not making any art," she smiles.

"Details," I wave my hand as if to dismiss this idea. "Call yourself an artist whether or not you produce a single piece of anything that anyone else might call 'art.' Your dreams are art enough if you choose to become the artist of your life and create with them, through them."

"Okay, but it's not the same."

"If you're an artist, in the sense that we think of 'artist'," I say, "like Picasso . . . then wild horses couldn't keep you from making 'art.' It's a wild-horse kind of drive to create when you're an artist, and it kills many an artist. Picasso, for example, made hundreds of sketches in preparation for *Les Demoiselles d'Avignon,* and he made art until the day he died, at 91, because he found ways to be with the wild horse-ness of it all. Constantly. Everywhere he went. And he trampled a lot of people while at it. But, like him, you would go mad with not making art if you were an artist in that sense. Or perhaps like, Van Gogh, you'd be eating tubes of oil paints, cutting off your ear, and crying out in anguish for all that is not finding a way to come through you."

"Perhaps I'm not an artist like that," she says quietly. "But I am crying out in anguish. Only it's a quiet, breathless cry that nobody can hear."

"Can you hear it?"

She nods. "But I try not to. I mostly try to drown it out. But . . . it's always there."

"Can you hear it now?"

She closes her eyes. Then, "Yes," she says.

"What does it sound like?"

There is a long silence. "Like my mother saying, 'Oh, don't worry about me,'" she says finally. "'I'm okay.'"

"But she's not okay?"

"She's on the floor with a broken hip," the dreamer says then. "No, she's not okay," she pauses. "And it's the sound of that—a lifetime of denial pressing against me." Another long silence. Then, "I don't want to end up like that, like her."

"As though?"

"As though she tried not to be here, or something. Or . . . I don't mean that she wasn't a good mother. She was. But as a woman, an individual, a human being—it's as though she thought it was bad or wrong or not right somehow to make a mark on things. *Her* mark. That it was wrong of her to have a mark even, let alone want to make it on the world. I know it was the influence of her cultural heritage, but it's as though she thought she had to sacrifice herself for us, for my sister and me. And at the end of her life she just became so tired . . . and, in that moment of her death, after she broke her hip, it's as though she just walked away from it all, just like the people in this dream town, and . . . I find this . . . well, really rather tragic," she says. "As though . . . she never lived up to her potential."

"So is it this feeling of perhaps not living up to your own potential that silently clamors from within?"

"And all the attendant fear," she nods. "And that's why I'm so relieved, I guess, with this message from Ell and Ell(y) . . . because it suggests . . . well . . . that it's . . . not too late."

"Isn't this why there's the sense of not being able to get there—to Ell and Ell(y)'s—any sooner? Because, even though there is no 'sooner,' as you say, the longing that things might be otherwise is awakened? So it's the being seen-into-being that Ell and Ell(y) offer, and your curiosity about what they 'see' in you, along with the place that they are holding for you, in dynamic tension with the silent clamor of your being and the attendant fear of not living up to your potential, along with the fated ancestral longing that things could have been different for your mother."

She nods.

"So it's here, precisely, in the space created by this dynamic tension that you want to enter, and ever enter as an orientation, as a way of making you an artist and a true lover of the world. So how you enter and care for this place—which is their place and your place and now your mother's even—matters."

"Because it's not really over there, down yonder in the South somewhere," she nods.

"Well, why do you imagine that the dream is set in the South?" I ask then.

"Isn't there something about the mythological directions?" she twists herself toward me as though her whole body is a question mark.

"Well, they say that West is where we go to begin things. East is where we go to end them. North is where we go to get into trouble. And South . . . South is where we go to find a friend."

"Oh," she says suddenly, her voice catching, as she places her hands over her heart. And, as her eyes well up with emotion, "That's exactly where my mother never went," she says then. "It wasn't her fault. She had that Northern immigrant Norwegian thing going on. So," she shrugs, "she didn't know any better. But it's as though . . . she . . . never befriended herself."

"Well, isn't that what's going on with the names?"

"Ell and Ell(y)?"

I nod.

"I'm so curious about the names," she says. "They strike me as 'her' and 'other her,' or 'she' and 'other she' with that enclosed (y) distinguishing the one from the other, though not in a diminutive sense, like a mother and daughter, or something. No, I get the strong sense that Ell and Ell(y) are a couple that just happen to have the same name."

"Isn't it because Ell and Ell (y) are 'she' and 'other she' enclosed within (y)ou? Aren't they . . . like Happy Head, divine images epiphanizing themselves? So they are not 'over there' outside of you in the South somewhere, or 'over there' in an 'other' world sense? Aren't they in the South . . . of you, in the hearth of your being, where you might go to find a friend? Aren't they, in fact, *you?* And in this way, isn't their nearness so excessive that at first it acts as a veil? And isn't this why you, like me, and like all us inexperienced ones, go looking for the Other outside, in the concrete world of things, in a desperate search from form to form?"

"The letters 'el' at the ends of names like 'Micha-el' and 'Rapha-el' and 'Gabri-el,' mean 'of God' in the Hebrew language," one of those gathered offers then. "It strikes me that 'Ell' and 'Ell(y)' are perhaps a feminized form 'of God' within you—and that they are doubled up in order to get your attention."

"Well, they've got it," the dreamer nods. "All I want to do is be there, in that house, with them . . . as presences."

"Speaking of doubling up . . . did you notice the doubling up in the dream, when you move from the backyard to the inside of the house? And then, as you look at the article on the front cover of the magazine, when you say, 'So I turn inside to find the story'? Gorgeously put, don't you agree?" I ask, looking around the room. "And then, turning inside, to the inside story, you go inside again, only deeper this time, into the storied, nesting-doll place that is being held for you—in your own body, and in the dreaming world by Ell and Ell(y). Beautiful!

"So you'll want to practice going inside, which, in the beginning will likely require a 'going' there—as though it's someplace 'other' than where you are already, because it's an orientational difference that takes practice. So you'll want to go South, to the hearth of your being, where you'll need to make friends with your will. So that with practice, and over time, the knack for how spirit enters will 'become as simple and ordinary as eating and drinking,' as Rumi reminds us."

She takes a deep breath.

"You'll want to practice the deep listening that Rumi encourages us to practice. For the patterns are always being forgotten—by you, by me, by all of us. So practice remembering them, and the love of the pattern that you and your soul twin chose together, and let this remember you into the realm of mystery and beauty and separation that is, as Rumi says, 'the unsayable absence.'

"And each and every time you go there, whether to put the dishes away, or to clean up the cracker crumbs, ask, with your whole body and being: *What is being asked of me now?* What capacities of soul am I being asked to develop?"

"And then get very quiet?"

"You can take some of your art supplies there and quietly practice with them. As a form of prayer. But try not to imagine that it's what you produce while you're there that is what's being asked of you. For art is merely what you love."

"So art is just a vehicle that helps me to remember that I came here to remember and display something?"

"And 'how' you do this will be the expansive gift that you'll want to offer the world," I nod. "Not your paintings, or your sculptures, or whatever you produce, though you are certainly welcome to offer those to the world, too."

"And what Ell and Ell(y) see in me will be revealed?"

"With any amount of grace," I nod. "Slowly. And it's this that, if we are at all lucky, you will offer to the rest of us."

She smiles. Then, "Do we need to talk about why I am so annoyed with my son?" she twists her mouth sideways.

"Well, isn't he just the stand-in for why you aren't able to turn to the inside story?" I shrug. Then, to those gathered, "Don't we all have any number of stand-ins waiting in the wings so that we might convince ourselves, and those around us, how we are unable to turn to the inside story?" Then, turning back to the dreamer, "So your son just helps you to see this, that's all."

"So I should really be annoyed with me," she adds.

"Just the lit-up part of you. That is, if you insist on being annoyed," I smile. "But now the dreamtime brings the twofold side of your being to the inside story anyway and opens up your longing to be in the precise place that's being held for you by Ell and Ell(y). So isn't our annoyance with ourselves just another one of the many distractions?"

"The work of love is always right before us," she nods.

"Maybe you couldn't have gotten there any sooner, but you can go there now, and now, and now, ever and always, so long as you are in a living body that's still incarnating into the world."

"So now that this has been revealed," the dreamer asks, "should I expect to encounter shame whenever I am falling into one of the distractions?"

"According to our old friend and mentor Plato, yes. But not so that you can put the hair vest on and get out the whip," I say, making then as though I am flagellating myself. "You are being loved into remembering who you are really for the sake of the world."

"So just get on with it," she says. "Get on with the project."

"If there's time and energy enough after you've spent a lifetime of loving afternoons tending to Ell and Ell(y)'s, and you still feel inclined to get out that hair vest and whip, well, then, knock yourself out. But all the beating up we do to ourselves, it seems, is just another one of the distractions. Just another clever, deceitful trick of the lit-up side of being. So . . . remind yourself that the work of love is always right before you and . . . get on with the work."

"Of love."

"The goal is to release this power of love—this same love that, for example, you experience so all-at-once at Ell and Ell(y)'s—into the world. So going to the inside story and developing into your potential not only has the power to transform you, it has the power to transform the world, or at least your little corner of it. For one thing, it changes your experience of time and your perception of the world. Yet, this is but preparation for the more mysterious work, that is, being ever more present to the force of love, which is not merely the feeling of love, but an active, conscious practice of finding our way into the interactive field of dreams and living in sympathy of being with the images we encounter there. So, in this case, Ell and Ell(y) and their home, the home that is now living in you, which, when you practice tending, makes you ever more capable of the God of your Being. That is, better able to hold experiences of dread and anger, anxiety and confusion, and all those things that take place between us and others that we usually try to avoid.

"So by making room for what's actually here, we become co-creators of the field of being, in the field—that same ever-changing field of dreams that the dreamtime is always inviting us to participate in. If we can learn to vividly participate in this interactive dreamtime field and then release the force of the love we gather there into the world, love then has the potential to become a transformative and moral force."

"And it's for this work of love that the dreamtime is so very interested in developing devotees?"

I nod. "When love and the imagination arrive, they invite us to change, to enter into our potential. In Ell and Ell(y)'s, what you feel so vividly, so all-at-once, is your coming-to-be, even though you have no idea where this will lead. But if you accept the invitation that Ell and Ell(y) offer, in an ongoing way . . ."

"As an orientation," she adds.

"As an orientation," I echo, "then there's the promise that they, too, will enter into their spiritual potential through you, through your living body and your ongoing willingness to give them another place to be. And what you will soon discover is the potential for soul-making through you, through the spiritual forces of Ell and Ell(y), and the undulating, all-at-once current in the house of being that, together, you now tend for the sake of the world coming into being."

So, though Mystical Poverty presents itself as the threshold of entry, there is nothing mystical about the practice of tending dreams this way. All we are doing, quite simply, is taking what's being given to us dream by dream, moment by moment, image by image, and lending ourselves bodily to the images for their sake, so that together we might make something beautiful and offer it to the dream of the world and the Earth's unfolding.

ADVENT DREAMING

Beauty becomes real through patience, through love and through the compassionate seeing into things—all of which need to be learned, and all of which the dreamtime endeavors, with patience, with love and compassion, to ever teach us. *Oh, why is it so hard for us moderns to imagine that we are loved?*

It is winter, and night, and dark in that northern sort of way. *Can you see the lake? It's there, just there, in the dark. Wait for it. Your eyes will adjust to the dark. Soon you'll begin to see what's been there all along.*

It's a dark, northern lake. And there is a dark . . . what? Presence? Yes, a dark someone stands at the lake. And now they—this dark presence, and the dark lake, and the dark of the night in the north, and even Winter herself wait for something or someone. *Is it me? You? Perhaps it is us?*

The next night, in the same dark dreaming place, the dark presence is there, too, still waiting, as though no time has passed from last night's dream to this night's. Everything, in fact, is the same, only now there's a large advent calendar at the center of the lake, with little doors that open to hidden treasures. But instead of the numbers going "one" through "twenty-four" in a right-to-left pattern, as they would, say, if we were reading a book, they swirl in a large circle around the center.

Feeling our way along in the luminous dark, following the numbered doors and spiraling our way into the center, we find two hidden treasures behind two of the last doors, though just what these treasures are cannot be recalled upon waking. It's not what's behind the doors that matter, therefore. What's essential is that there are little doors at the center of things behind which hidden treasures wait to be found by us.

The next night, in the center of that same advent calendar, an entire room is revealed. And though there is nothing about this central room that says "beautiful" or "sacred" in the plain-view-way it appears—it doesn't have stained glass windows, or windows at all, for that matter. It's non-descript, rather like a conference room—it's undeniably beautiful and utterly sacred. And not just because it's a hidden room at the center of things, but because it also includes the treasured experience of getting here.

Standing in this treasure room, treasured now too, a rose suddenly roses between us, between you and me, sacred-heart-red, large and living and lit-from-within, and yet somehow still dark, and so velvety soft to the touch. *Oh, can you feel it?* It's ever so delicate and yet wildly fragrant.

And lifted up through the ages by the dream of this rosing beauty, slowly and sweetly, at long last we awaken to all that the soul saw when once it looked out upon the world and saw reality. And wholly remembered then, loved into being fully-winged and weightless once again, we are returned to the center of the opening rose, ever dreaming the whole thing into being.

ENDNOTES

1 Rainer Maria Rilke, *Selected Poems of Rainer Maria Rilke*, Robert Bly, trans., (New York: Harper Perennial, 1981), 60

2 Nakhshabī, *Juẓ'iyāt o Kulliyāt*, (London: British Library, India Office Collection, Islamic 905), 156

3 Perhaps this sentence should read, "Well, what *white* almost-six-year-old wouldn't adore seeing dapper Rex Harrison interact with all those exotic animals in such a sophisticated and sympathetic way?" Even though I am not wholly white, I was mostly raised as a mostly white girl in a mostly white world. Subsequent viewing of *Doctor Dolittle* reveals just how racist the world I grew up in was (and perhaps is still).

4 James Hillman, *The Thought of the Heart and the Soul of the World* (Woodstock: Spring Publications, 1995), 6

5 Crockett Johnson, *Harold and the Purple Crayon* (New York: HarperCollins, 1955)

6 Coleman Barks, trans., *The Essential Rumi* (New York: HarperCollins, 2004), 113

7 Robert Sardello, *Concerning the Everyday Life of Soul*, 2000-2007, http://www.spiritualschool.org/articles_everyday.htm

8 Henry Corbin, *The Man of Light in Iranian Sufism* (New Lebanon: Omega Publications, 1994), 112

9 Thomas Mann, *The Magic Mountain*, John E. Woods, trans., (New York: Random House / Vintage 1995), 495

10 Antonio Machado, *Times Alone: Selected Poems of Antonio Machado*, Robert Bly, trans., (Middletown: Wesleyan University Press, 1983), 57

11 Marie Howe, *The Kingdom of Ordinary Time* (New York: W. W. Norton & Company, 2009), 43

12 John Moyne and Coleman Barks, *Say I am You Rumi: Poetry Interspersed with Stories of Rumi and Shams* (Athens: MAYPOP, 1994), 116

13 e.e. cummings, *A Miscelleny* (New York: October House, 1965), 335

14 Daniel Ladinsky, trans., *The Gift: Poems by Hafiz, The Great Sufi Master* (New York: Penguin Compass, 1999), 276

15 William Stafford, *Even in Quiet Places*, (Lewiston: Confluence Press, 2010), 8

16 Coleman Barks, trans., *The Essential Rumi* (New York: HarperCollins, 2004), 155

17 Daniel Ladinsky, trans., *The Gift: Poems by Hafiz, The Great Sufi Master* (New York: Penguin Compass, 1999), 330

APPENDIX

Practices for Remembering Dreams

1. Name your willingness and desire to participate in and remember the images in your dreams as you prepare yourself for bed each night.
2. Stay in liminal space if at all possible for five minutes each morning—this is the most important time for doing dream work. The word "liminal" means threshold—it's where we get the word "subliminal," which means "below the threshold." So liminal space is that space between dreaming and waking—when we are awakened to the story written inside.
3. Keep your eyes closed.
4. Try to stay in the same body position you awoke in.
5. Patiently cast your line and fish with receptive expectation.
6. Don't give up. It's a practice, and like all practices, you will eventually be rewarded with results. This is like building a muscle or like learning an instrument. It's all about showing up for practice.
7. Give your dream a title. Start from what you can remember (this is especially helpful if you get up to use the washroom in the middle of the night!).
8. Don't discard an image because it seems like a "nothing" image. No image is too small to work with. They all have the same weight as far as psyche is concerned. Refrain from judging your dreams by their contents.
9. Keep a journal. Write or draw your dreams in it, even if they are only felt-senses, or moods upon waking. And if you decide to draw them, refrain from judging the results of your efforts. Remember, it's all about showing up, about letting those on the other side—the weavers of dreams—know that you're awake and watching, listening, *being*, even while sleeping.

Recommended Reading

Stephen Aizenstat, *Dream Tending*
Owen Barfield, *Romanticism Comes of Age*
Martin Buber, *Eclipse of God*
Joseph Campbell, *Pathways to Bliss*
The writings of Tom Cheetham
The writings of Henry Corbin
Robert Earl Cushman, *Therapeia*
Dante, *The Divine Comedy*
The writings of Christine Downing
The poetry of Hafiz
The writings of James Hillman
Homer, *The Odyssey*
Crockett Johnson, *Harold and the Purple Crayon*
The writings of Peter Kingsley
The writings and poetry of D.H. Lawrence
Kristofor Minta and Herbert Pföstl, *to die no more*
The poetry of Pablo Neruda
The poetry of Mary Oliver
The writings and poetry of Rainer Maria Rilke
The poetry of Rumi
The writings of Robert Sardello
The poetry of William Stafford

About the Author

Born and raised in Saskatoon, Saskatchewan, Canada, Renée Coleman lives with her husband and their four children in Santa Clarita, California, where she works at developing the art and practice of dream-centered living. As a certified DreamTender, she endeavors to teach dreamers how to navigate through the many twists and turns of the dreamtime using a holistic, embodied, and imaginal approach.

Renée earned her Mythological Studies doctorate (with an emphasis on Depth Psychology) at Pacifica Graduate Institute in 2002. Before that, while living in New York and later in Los Angeles, she worked as a model and actor, appearing in many films, television programs, and commercials. *Icons of a Dreaming Heart* is her first book.

Made in the USA
Charleston, SC
22 October 2015